I think it's cool when authors have endorsements from big names and impressive people. That is a great indicator to the reader if they will enjoy the book. However, I wanted to get review from my ladies, my friends, my readers-- because they are everyday women just like you and me. And quite honestly, that's who I wrote this book for. So I want you to be able to see what women just like you are saying about this book. I love muh girls! <3

xo, Holly

"When you know Holly, there are some things you can always count on: Laughter, Transparency, and an unwavering faith in her Savior. "Joy is My Jam" is classic Holly Mutlu. At times silly and quirky; and at others raw and gut-level honest. All while consistently, repeatedly pointing the reader to Christ - the true source of our Joy! Holly - I just can't believe you wrote an entire book without mentioning Ranch Dressing one single time!"

Beth Warren

"Hilariously serious! A relatable book of personal stories that teach us to recognize God's movement and presence in all areas of our lives. How to dance our pain into joy!"

Stephanie Jones

"I could relate to every word! It's like we have been best friends for years and she knew exactly what I needed to hear."

Lara Buechler

"Wonderful, inspiring! I can't wait to get my hands on the whole thing. You brought Joy into my Jam just by sharing."

Kari

"Just being able to have a sneak peak of this book was amazing. I am so excited to read it in its entirety and see how much more it can touch my life. Knowing that we can have Joy no matter what life throws our way is a great feeling."

Amy Baker

"I want a book that can take me from teaching me about how God working in our lives to making me laugh at myself, because at some point in our lives have had a great time on the dance floor."

Colleen Eidemiller

"A great mixture of inspiration and truth, sprinkled with some comedy. It's like reading a book in the form of girls night out with your best friends. Laugh until ya pee a little."

Janice Buckley

"Holly Mutlu is a writer who brings authenticity, humor, and Godly scripture to every word of her writing. Joy is my Jam is a book for all women looking for Godly wisdom but also humor at laughing at yourself. She will be your best friend but will also tell it to you straight with some Godly truth."

Ally Ross

"The words Holly wrote hold so much truth, boldness, faithfulness. My tank is full after reading Joy is My Jam."

Melissa H.

"Joy is my Jam" is incredible!!! It's, well, THE JAM!! Holly has a way of laying things out in a way that we all can relate to! Have you ever spoken to therapist, a pastor, or anyone for that matter, and thought..."they don't get it, they haven't been there" ? I know I have. Look no further... she gets it! She openly shares her own struggles in a raw (and sometimes hilarious) way, and breaks it down to truth! GODS LOVING TRUTH! Holly has personally helped me through some of my life's struggles. Things I didn't want to face, or even tell others. No judgements, just love. She is truly one of a kind, and so is this book! A definite must read! GET YOUR JOY BACK!!! Every single one of you deserves it."

Robin Cascone

"Recapture your joy with Holly's totally transparent and funny life experiences. Reading this book will allow you to make sense of your pain, allowing it to become your catalyst into true joy! A must read for all women!"

Joy Hoover

"'Joy is My Jam' is an incredibly authentic book that really helps you understand the importance of perspective. Holly Mutlu tells it like it is in the most genuine, kind, and hilarious way. God's love is woven throughout the pages and the world must read it!"

Sarah Chaney

"Joy Is My Jam is raw, honest and encouraging. It will have you crying, nodding your head one minute then laughing, saying, "yes girl!" the next. Relatable on so many levels, it sometimes felt like I was looking in a mirror."

Robin Carney

"Serious but, rolling on the floor laughing funny!!! You are so right, God's plan for what we encounter in life is for us to learn and grow. We can all relate to having little accidents, but you handled them superbly! #joyismyjam!"

Rosa Pena

Joy Is My Jam

Holly Mutlu

DEDICATION

This book is for all my everyday ladies. I'm guessing that you've had one of those seasons in life where you're smiling on the outside and yet hurting deeply on the inside. People assume that because you're laughing, you're joyful. The laughter not only numbs the pain but it helps to cover it. My prayer sweet sister is that you will discover true joy as you read these pages and that your laughter no longer disguises your pain but becomes a true reflection of your heart.

CONTENTS

Introduction

Hey gurrrrl!

I've always wanted to write a book. But, never in a million years did I think I would, because I didn't believe I could. My lack of belief was the lid to my own limitations. So, I took the lid off and here we are. My goal in this book is to help you take the lid off of your life so you can live a life of joy no matter where you find yourself today. No matter what your situation looks or even feels like, I want you to still find joy.

Speaking of lids, you know when you take a two liter bottle of soda and shake it to high heavens, then open it up to have it spray all over the place? (I'm not the only one who has done this, right?) That's what it kinda felt like as I was writing this book. Fortunately, I've had an amazing team who have been placed around me, and who slowed me down a bit so it didn't feel like a big, sticky, carbonated mess coming at ya all at once. They helped me slowly open the container and seep the air out to access the goodness in the bottle without making a mess!

Now about this book - This is me. While each chapter is a story on its own, they are all a piece of me. Sure, you could use the word complex to describe this book, but instead of that, I'm going to use the word multi-dimensional, because that's more like it. I'm going to share from every aspect of who I am. A believer, a mom, a wife, a sister, a counselor, a friend, a life coach, a preacher, and a bold, sometimes edgy woman!

I want to encourage you to be your true authentic self, the person that God uniquely created to make an impact on this world. Whether you realize it or not, you're leaving your mark on every single person you come in contact with and that's POWERFUL! Since I am encouraging you to be yourself in all your beauty, flaws, and gloriousness, I decided to write in that same way. So in these pages are the words of my personal, my professional, and all of my crazy self!

At the end of the day, I don't want this book to just light a fire and inspire something in you, I want this book to help change you into a better version of yourself—so you can operate at a higher level while embracing your true you. I know that information alone doesn't bring about change. It's really the application. So here's my simple formula for the book.

Information (my stories) + Application (the how to's) = Transformation (positive change)

Since I'm no math guru I had to keep this formula super simple. I'm keeping the formula simple with the hope of not just inspiring you, but also giving you tools to tuck away in a pretty little pink glittery tool box that you can take out and use to create a joyful and sparkly life.

Ok sister, it's time to do this thang!

Chapter 1

Feelings Are Like Toddlers

If You Don't Train Them, They Will Train You

Oh, the joys of a toddler. The hugs, kisses, and snuggles are priceless. And the giggles— so contagious. And then there's the temper tantrum. It's inevitable. It takes superhuman strength to go up against the mighty temper tantrum. Like Wonder Woman vs Ares. In other words, it's a full on battle.

The thing is, when it first happens, you don't realize you need superpower strength to battle the temper tantrum. You're not prepared for battle because a little body couldn't possibly have more strength than you, could it? This cute and joyful little being couldn't possibly bring the whole household down in a matter of minutes could they?

And then it happens for the first time.

I remember the first time I experienced the mighty blow that comes from a toddler's tantrum. There I was, standing in the kitchen, when my two-and-a-half year old son wanted something to drink. Thinking nothing of it, I went to the cupboard, grabbed his red cup and just as I was about to fill it with juice, he began to whine, "Noooooooo Mama! I unt bew cup."

"Oh, buddy the blue cup is dirty, this red one will be just fine. It's the same apple juice, it's not a big deal," I tenderly replied. Oh, those famous last words. You see, in toddler land, the idea that the wrong color cup is "not a big deal" simply does not compute. It's actually the end of the world.

It was like Satan's spawn came out from nowhere. His head spun like the exorcist, and all of the sudden he screamed like nobody's business. I frantically scurried around the kitchen looking for the blue plastic cup, because clearly that's what I needed to get him in order to settle him down.

Eventually I found the special blue cup, washed it out, poured the juice, and handed him the cup. The minute he saw the blue cup, the demon that had possessed him, left, and my little sweet angel of a toddler stood there with a smile on his face.

In that moment, this little mind, who could barely put together a sentence, had won. Even though he didn't have the best communication skills, his emotional explosion was so great that I allowed him to dictate the situation.

As any mother knows, temper tantrums are never just one-time occurrences. After countless times of giving in to this tiny toddler's demands, it began to wear on me. I couldn't keep up. I was getting drained and I was tired of dealing with the craziness and instability of never knowing what would set him off.

One day, it happened again, but much much worse. No matter the color of cup I chose, it was never the right one. It wasn't good enough. I ran around the kitchen like a madwoman and as my strong two-and-a-half foot tall dictator followed me around, I realized in that moment, that something needed to change. This little knee-high dude was making his every demand known, and bossing me around. I was doing everything I could to please him, and yet it was not my job to please him. It was my duty to teach him. I realized in that moment that if I didn't teach him, he would walk around the rest of his life unfulfilled and always wanting more.

Of course, that begs the question, how can I effectively train him when he's the one who's got me trained? Unbeknownst to me, that little adorable dude had manipulated me and had me exactly where he wanted me. I realized that if I didn't change something soon, it would only grow worse with time. As a mom of not only a toddler, but also two teens at the time, I knew that the days go by loooooong, yet the years are short.

3

I committed to making a shift in the dynamics of this relationship, so that I wouldn't blink and find my baby had grown into a teenager who threw fits until he got his way. There is a Proverb that says, "Train up a child in the way he should go, and when he is old he won't depart." Sure, in the moment, he would want "his way," but if left unchecked, his fits would only become more demanding and they'd set him up for a life of unfulfilled expectancy and entitlement. The mere thought of that was enough to give me the strength to begin to change the hierarchy in the relationship.

I learned that as soon as I saw a glimpse of Ares, I must do my Wonder Woman spin and prepare for battle. That's the only way to win against a toddler. You must be more strong-willed than they are. Quite honestly, it takes supernatural power to do so. I say it off the cuff like it's no big deal, but it is legit the most emotionally draining battle you face early on as a mother. Trust me, I know. It's why so many moms just give in and search for the right color cup. Fighting against the temper tantrum is no easy task, but it is oh so important.

We must not allow the noise of the temper tantrum to drown out the voice of wisdom.

Do you realize that you have your own temper tantrums? Sure, you might have gotten more sophisticated and perhaps you don't throw full on fits anymore, but if your feelings are dictating your life, then you, my friend, are allowing your feelings to run the show.

Perhaps right now you find yourself in a place where your feelings are dictating your life, just like a toddler dictates which cup he wants. Maybe you feel like you need a new house in order to make you happy. So, you get the house, and yet it's not good enough. You feel like the other color cup will make you happy, so you get the new car. Nope. Still empty. So you continue to search until you feel something that satisfies...and the search continues on and on.

Let me lay it all out here for you. YOU have the power and authority over your feelings (even if it feels like they are controlling you). Trust me on this. Most people allow their feelings to act as their GPS, guiding them to their destination. As their feelings change, so does their destination, when in fact our feelings were not created to be our navigational system. They were created to be more like a gauge, a "check engine light" if you will. The check engine light tells us there is something going on under the hood that needs to be addressed. Sometimes it's simply routine maintenance, and other times it's a blown engine. If it's a blown engine, it's likely because the driver has been paying more attention to the GPS than to the check engine light.

In the next chapter I'm going to geek out and show you how you can begin to train your feelings. Just a heads up, this exercise is a lot like the toddler, in that, the more you've been catering to him, the more difficult it is to change. However, it's not impossible and it is totally worth it. You'll just need to be aware of the supernatural strength (Thank you, Holy Spirit!) you have within you, who will help fight this battle for you.

APPLICATION

I think we all get to that point like I was with my son, where we say enough is enough! So let's look at that verse again, "Train up your child in the way she should go, and when she is old she won't depart". What about your inner child? That's who you need to train. Decide that you are going to will against the temper-tantrum throwing toddler inside of you and train her up right! Be willing to dig deep, even though it's going to hurt a little, to see what is causing all the frustration. Then take time to ask the Holy Spirit to give you His supernatural strength to fight this battle, in order that you mature into woman God is calling your to be.

Now let's make it personal…

Ask yourself if you are willing to be honest about your feelings and your tantrums. If so, then let's get ready to rock this!

In the next section you will learn what to do with them once they've been identified.

What are some feelings that have dictated your life?

Where do you feel yourself coming up empty?

Is there a situation that continuously arises in your life that you have surrendered your feelings to?

What is that situation?

Are you ready to take charge over your feelings to find a more joyful life? Then let's read on sister.

Chapter 2

The Label Maker

Processing Your Emotions

Inside of you, every moment of every day, evaluating every situation, is your very own personal label maker. Just like the label maker you use to label canisters of food, moving boxes, or your kid's toy boxes, this label maker is constantly printing out labels. However, when it comes to your internal label maker, there are just two labels it makes: good or bad. Thing is, that label maker is about as wise as that two-and-a half-year-old toddler from the last chapter. It might know how to manipulate, but it does not have true wisdom.

You may not even realize it, but your subconscious is filtering everything through the lens of either good or bad and then labeling as such. Your label maker has a vast amount of control over the joy in your life as you label every person, every situation, every moment, and everything in your life one or the other. Good or bad.

Left to its own devices, just like the toddler, this label maker will go into self-centered mode and become very destructive. Also, just like the toddler, this label maker, once trained properly, is a huge blessing in your life.

Letting your label maker run on autopilot is about as dangerous as letting your toddler make decisions for the whole household. Yet, that's what so many people unknowingly do.

It seems crazy to let something with so much power over your life run on autopilot without a second thought, doesn't it?

However, today can be the day. The day that you turn your label maker off of toddler-like autopilot and begin to run that machine for yourself. When you do this, the amount of joy in your life can be unlimited.

Here's where I begin to geek out and start getting into the deets of how this goes down. I'm going to try to keep it as simple as possible, because I could go on forever about this juicy stuff. Bear with me as I proudly tap into my inner nerd and guide you through this. If you're a fellow nerd, I dedicate this next section to you.

EMOTIONS

Our emotions were created to benefit us. They serve a positive purpose. Just like a toddler, when left to their own devices they can run out of control and can become very destructive.

Emotions are instinctive. They are reactive based upon an external situation. While there is a physiological response (i.e. anger or fear releases adrenaline that will increase the heart rate, tighten muscles, increase mental alertness, etc.) the actual emotion is only felt for a short time. From there, we develop an array of feelings as a result of the process our minds take us through. Part of that process includes the label maker.

In between the instinctive emotion and feelings, are several layers. I'm going to nerd out even more so now and go into some details that are going to be game changers for you.

To start with, you have an external situation, and this situation evokes an instinctive emotion.

Whether or not you realize it, you are labeling that external situation either good or bad. From there, you will send everything through either a good or bad filter based upon the label your mind automatically created for it.

Next, you begin to think thoughts about the situation, and your thoughts will fall in line with the label you gave the particular situation.

If the situation was labeled good, you will have good thoughts. If the situation was labeled bad, you will have negative thoughts.

These thoughts then play out in your mind. As the thoughts go through your head, your feelings are created. And yup, you guessed it, if the thoughts are good, then your feelings will be good. If the thoughts are bad, the feelings will be bad.

Now let's take it a step further to prevent your emotions from doing the equivalent of the two-year-old's temper tantrum.

Your feelings dictate your mood, which then dictates your behavior, which results in a new situation, which will be either good or bad depending on that original label.

I'm going to get really vulnerable here and share a personal story to demonstrate how you can use your label maker in a way that makes life more joyful.

Check out this chart:

EXTERNAL SITUATION
↓
INSTINCTIVE EMOTIONAL RESPONSE
↓
INTERPRETATION FILTER
↙ ↘
POSITIVE   NEGATIVE
THOUGHT PROCESS
↓
FEELINGS
↓
ACTIONS
↓
NEW EXTERNAL SITUATION

I'm going to get really vulnerable here and share a personal story to demonstrate how you can use your label maker in a way that makes life more joyful.

As we break it down, I want to show you how this works.

External Situation: The death of my father-in-law.

My father-in-law "Baba" (which is Turkish for dad) was an amazing man. I always adored him and cherished him. Baba was one of the sweetest men I have ever known (my husband is one of them as well, clearly the apple doesn't fall far from the tree). Over the years, my in-laws became another set of parents for me, who were always there for me no matter what. I'd like to think I was there for them as well.

So when my always healthy father-in-law became ill and rapidly declined, it was a shock for all of us. I flew down to Florida to be at his bedside. At eighty-three he had diabetes, but other than that, he was as healthy as a horse. Then, one day he went into the hospital. He was in and out of the ICU for about thirty days before his passing.

So although he was elderly, he was in good health. Which is why his passing was totally unexpected.

Emotion: My instinctive emotional reaction was sadness.

Sadness. This was a tremendous loss to our family. I was going to miss my sweet Baba's laughter and his ability to light up a room. He was always a happy cheerful fella—a natural comedian. While not a pro, his delivery was as good as any of the top comedians I'd ever seen. And while his jokes were often inappropriate, I knew I was going to miss them and the joy he brought to the world. I was sad. Very sad.

It's important to know that every emotion serves a purpose. Sadness serves to make us realize that there is something we love that is hurt, lost, or gone. The purpose of sadness helps us understand the beauty of what once was.

Label Maker: Looking beneath the obvious and seeing the good, or to be more accurate, trusting God in the midst of your situation.

When you become aware of the label maker you realize it's truly a fight of Spirit (good) vs. Flesh (bad).

Our natural instinct is to send most things through our flesh and see things in a negative light. When the label maker is left on autopilot that's pretty much what happens. Most things are labeled as bad.

But when you choose to look past your flesh and those intense emotions and see things through the Spirit, you have the ability to see the good in all things.

14

Even if you don't see the good, you have the faith to know there will be good that comes out of it.

Of course I was sad over the passing of Baba. He was a great loss and it left an emptiness in our hearts. This emptiness is where grief comes in. I allowed myself to go through the typical grieving process. We must go through grieving and yet not get stuck there. So, rather than labeling this situation as bad and looking through the eyes of my flesh, I decided to look through the eyes of the Holy Spirit and see the good. Baba's smile and laughter lit up this earth for eighty-three years. He was an ob-gyn and throughout his career, he delivered over 6,000 babies. What a gift that was to thousands of families. He was tender hearted and sweet, a gentle soul. I was blessed to have him as a strong fixture in my life for nineteen years.

Having my label maker create a positive label for Baba's life created positive thoughts.

Thoughts: What an awesome man! He left an amazing legacy and I want to leave one as well.

When you've got a positive label, your thoughts are now geared in a positive direction. Now, I began to think about the legacy Baba left behind. One of joy. One of love and making the most ordinary moments extraordinary. I began thinking about all the things Baba did. With very little money and broken English, he came to the USA with my precious mother-in-law and created an amazing life for the two of them and their three boys. They fought through adversity and overcame struggles. They traveled, they celebrated, they lived fully and happily. And at the end of the day, it all happened so fast. The scripture, "life is but a vapor" was more real to me now than it had ever been. And thinking about how quickly life flies by, how much Baba did in his life, and how he lived vivaciously and courageously, well, it made me begin to reflect on my life. Where was I not stepping out? Where was I holding back in life? How could I really begin to live a life of fullness? To truly live out loud?

Feelings: An urgency to begin living life to the fullest.

With the realization of the full life Baba lived, and how quickly it had passed, came a new birth in my soul. It stirred something inside my spirit. Something that had been dormant in my soul, began to come alive! That fiery flame of zest that, in my youth, burned bright was catching fire once again. I was feeling the urgency to live life to the fullest. An urgency to quit living inside my comfortable little shell of a world and get out and explore. I knew I was created for more. More than getting caught up in the minutiae of life— the bills, the cleaning, and the day-to-day responsibilities. Yes, I'm still responsible for those things, but there is more to life than just existing in the day-to-day tasks. I wanted to pursue a better marriage, be a better mom, love bigger and louder than ever before. And more than anything, be a bigger mouthpiece for Christ— whatever that

16

looked like. With the realization of how short life truly is, I felt more than ever I needed to pursue that passion that God placed in my spirit as a young child.

Actions: Doing things scared.

At this point, my on and off again battle with anxiety was still somewhat private. That drive to pursue God more and to walk in my calling was so great that I knew that "no weapon formed against me would prosper", including fear. No longer was I bowing down to fear and allowing it to paralyze me. The fear in me began to bow down to the Holy Spirit in me, and I began to truly live. I slowly, very slowly, made changes that I had known needed to be made. I knew I couldn't pursue this "thing" (whatever it was) while still in my current position at the church (I was associate pastor). I was scared to death that my leaving would somehow hurt my pastor, his wife, and the church. My fear was a church split (people get weird when change happens in leadership). But God honored my obedient heart. He created a way that would phase me out of my position at the church, and into this new endeavor He was calling me to. It was slow, and I'm gonna be honest, at times it was painful, and often I was scared to death. However, I knew that if there was ever a time to step out, it was now. I was not going to allow fear to keep me from my purpose. I had to remind the fear in me to fear the God in me.

A New External Situation: Identified my purpose.

My original External Situation was a devastating loss. But when the worst heartbreak is labeled something "good" we are able to see beauty in even our darkest hour. God truly does create beauty from ashes...when we allow Him to.

I want to clarify that I'm not urging you not to feel your emotions— we must feel them because they each serve a very healthy purpose. My goal is to help you move forward after you've initially felt the emotion, so you don't get stuck in the flesh aspect of emotion but rather walk in the spiritual purpose of emotion.

I'm still working at this thing...I've not yet perfected it. I'm still fighting my flesh daily and trying to label all things through the eyes of the Spirit. Fortunately, in this situation of losing my father-in-law, I was able to see things beyond my natural flesh and to see them through the eyes of the Spirit. Which, in turn, created positive thoughts, positive feelings, positive actions, and now a brand new external situation— Knowing my purpose. From here I will send every aspect of my purpose through the label-making process. My prayer is that no matter what comes my way, I'll be able to label it properly, according to my Heavenly Father's will and not my own.

Before I go into the application portion of the chapter, I want to share this one last thought.

Baba and I would go out on dinner dates. In those times he gifted me with many memories, lots of laughter, words of encouragement, and wisdom. Every moment with Baba was a gift. And our last moments together were no different. He gifted me a new lease on life, new zeal and a fresh passion for pursuing God. Baba, I know you're probably busy right now, but thank you for leaving me that last precious gift. I love you!

APPLICATION

Intentionally apply the Label Maker and make it work for you.

Your Situation:

_____

Your Emotional Reaction:

_____ Anger _____Fear _____Sadness _____Joy

What Truth is that Emotion indicating?

_____
_____
_____
_____
_____

19

Choose Your Label:

_____ Positive _____ Negative

The negative thoughts you want to take captive of and get rid of— don't get too detailed, just acknowledge them and then fight them with truths:

_____
_____
_____
_____

The truths that feed your soul & nurture a positive resolution (Phil 4:8):

_____
_____
_____
_____
_____
_____
_____

The feelings that are created by the truths (be as detailed as possible):

_____
_____
_____
_____

_____

_____

_____

_____

The new situation now created is:

_____

_____

_____

_____

_____

_____

Let's make it more personal...

What are some situations (current or past) in your life that you've labeled as bad? Were the results from those situations negative?

Can you see where your thought process could have changed your perception and then the outcome?

What is at least one tangible step you can take the next time you realize your label maker is on autopilot, to prevent a negative outcome?

Ponder this: "To all who mourn in Israel, he will give a crown of beauty for ashes, a joyous blessing instead of mourning, festive praise instead of despair. In their righteousness, they will be like great oaks that the LORD has planted for his own glory" Isaiah 61:3. To those who were mourning (not those who were pretending everything was ok) he brought transformation and growth! That's what he desire is to do in your life, too!

Chapter 3

Be Careful Little Mouth What You Say

Taming the Tongue

Remember singing this Bible song as a child?

Be careful little eyes what you see

Be careful little ears what you hear

Be careful little mouth what you say

It's your words that pave the way.

Which direction do you want to go today?

(Yo, I'm rapping now!)

Growing up, I was one of seven kids. If you want the full back story, my mom and dad had five kids, they divorced, my dad remarried, and had two more. Now to me, half or full, they are still my siblings. But I feel the need to clarify, just so that in the future when I share about my family, you've got the full scoop. My mom later remarried in my adult years and I have step siblings with my stepfather's family but we didn't grow up together (however, they are still fam).

Anyway, we were and probably still are one of the most functional, dysfunctional families. I mean, if nothing else, we put the fun in dysfunction!

A super cool fact is that I have a twin. Short story long, we are considered identical, however we don't really look alike. We look like sisters, but not like twins. All my life, we've said we were identical because two out of three tests done at birth said we were identical (we're in a medical journal somewhere because, well, we liked to cause trouble wherever we went, and still do to this day.)

So anyway, while we are twins, we don't look much alike. She was always the "skinny" one and I was always the "chunky" one. Her name is Heidi and we had an uncle that used to come up to me at family reunions and say, "Ohhhhh you must be Holly— the round face has the O in her name." One more reminder that Heidi was skinnier than me.

I really wanted to be like Heidi. She was funny, outgoing, athletic, popular, pretty, and well, skinny. Obviously, I wanted to be skinny too and while I wasn't overweight by any means, I was constantly compared to

Heidi (that's what happens when you're a twin) and so I was made to feel a little insecure about the whole thing.

I remember once when I was probably around nine or ten, a well-intended loved one told me that I should suck in my stomach, and showed me how to hold it in so that I didn't have such a big belly. She said it would really help me look much better and skinnier.

Another loved one (who was an adult) offered me some of their clothes because they were "too small" for them and thought they'd be a good fit for me. And this person was actually quite a bit larger than I was.

These were all simple words- not said with any sort of malice behind them, and yet they were very painful.

Then there was the name calling at school- fat, the chunky one, or the chubby sister. I should probably mention my older sister was the "It" girl in her grade, and that my mom was considered the hot mom among many of my classmates.

So there I was, surrounded by what seemed like a lot of thin beauty, and then there was me.

The words kept coming over the years. The boys all liked my sisters and commented about my mom. And again, I truly don't believe anything was ever said or done out of anger or hate, they were all just facts.

But the words had power. And they caused a lot of pain. Pain that I tried to keep hidden or laughed off.

Fast forward a few years. Heidi was playing basketball and doing her sports thing. Heather was still hot as ever and that never stopped. My youngest sister Rachel was just a toddler so there was no comparison there (thank goodness!). And it was time for me to begin to figure out my identity.

I sucked at sports. I wasn't and am still not naturally athletic, well, not really. My husband will tell me he thinks I'm athletic but I think he does it just because he is trying to be kind. It felt like my sisters were killing it at this teen life and I was just getting by. During my freshman year, Heidi and I went out for cheerleading, and we both made freshmen squad. I hated it. I was at that awkward stage where I was just getting armpit hair, but not enough to shave, and if I shaved it looked like I didn't have any armpit hair, and so I would get made fun of for that.

And then do I even begin to mention how self-conscious I was in the cheerleading uniform? I will say that at this point I wasn't so quiet anymore. I had developed a reputation as the one with the "great personality." That flies over really well as a fourteen-year-old.

In junior high I had taken a liking to choir and since I was a big mouth I could sing really loudly. My music teacher encouraged me to go out for show choir. This was back before "Glee" or any of those type of shows, but it was actually cool to be in show choir. And it was kind of an honor to get in as a freshman. I was one of the few freshman that made it.

My choir director, Mr. Scothorn, saw something in me that I didn't see in myself. And I'll never forget what he said to me...He may not even remember it but these words were powerful to me.

He said, "Holly, it's time that you quit looking at what your sister has that you don't, and start looking at what you have and start to work with it."

Words have power. As much negativity as I had heard over the years about my weight, all it took was for one person to believe in me and convince me to start believing in myself.

That man spent time from the summer before my freshman year until the end of my senior year, investing in me. He would encourage me to step out, to try harder, to think bigger, to live larger, and to believe that I was a gift to this world.

Now, he also had to give me Saturday school because I broke a few rules. I totally thought I was his favorite and would be able to get away with it, but I quickly learned that I was not above the law. I did my Saturday school (and my detentions here and there) but it didn't affect my confidence. In fact, I believe the reason why I got into trouble was because my confidence was soaring and I truly believed I could get away with anything. Mr. Scothorn also taught me that rules were rules, and even if I thought they were meant to be broken, there would be consequences.

All it took was for one person to see where I was hurting and to invest in me, to find the beauty and giftings in me, and help bring them to the surface so I could see them. I'm forever grateful to Mr. Scothorn. God used him to make a massive impact on my life as he used the power of words for good.

He was living out Eph 4:29, "...Let everything you say be good and helpful, so that your words will be an encouragement to those who hear them."

And because he did that, my life was forever changed.

Over the years I've observed a few truths. One of them is this - hurting people hurt people. Healthy people heal people.

Are you healthy or hurting? Maybe it depends on who you're around. Around some people you are perfectly healthy, and around others you're hurting.

Luke 6:45 says, "The good person out of the good treasure of his heart produces good, and the evil person out of his evil treasure produces evil, for out of the abundance of the heart his mouth speaks." (ESV)

Your words will reveal the state of your heart— hurting or healing.

When I was about thirteen, my twin and I took our friend to a neighbor's house because the neighbor had this awesome horse and we wanted to go for a ride. I gotta be honest, I don't remember if either my twin or my friend rode the horse. I just remember my ride.

I was both a little nervous and looking forward to the ride at the same time. The neighbor trained this horse and it was a good horse, so I knew I was in good hands. However, what I didn't realize was the saddle was on a little loose.

The horse had a bit in its mouth and if you don't know anything about horses let me just share that the bit is how you control the direction of a horse. Now this horse seemed mammoth to me. It seemed gigantuous and I couldn't believe that I could control the movement of this entire horse simply by the reins that were attached to the bit in its mouth. So basically by directing the mouth, you controlled the whole horse.

I clearly didn't pay much attention to instruction because this horse just took off and I couldn't get the reins under control. It started galloping, which at first I'm sure looked a little funny. However, I'm guessing that my face started to get a bit panicky looking before too long. The more the horse ran, the more the saddle started to slide off to the side. Since the saddle was sliding down the left side of the horse, I began leaning to the right side to prevent from sliding more. However, because there was no tightening of the reins, which meant no direction in the mouth, the horse was taking off even faster!

The next part was and is still a big ole blur. I'm pretty sure I slid off the side of the horse and I remember feeling like the horse was going to trample me. Luckily for me, I somehow dove off to the side as I was falling from the saddle. I rolled over and out of the way. I was so shaken up that I was freaking out. I was trying to keep from bawling when I looked over at my sister, my friend, and my neighbor, who were all doubled over in laughter. My near death experience (ok that may be a bit of an exaggeration but it's how it felt), was their greatest entertainment that day.

Do you know how that "near death" experience began? It all started with a lack of control of the mouth. That disastrous horse riding experience was all because I couldn't control the mouth of that horse.

James 3:2 "For we all stumble in many ways. And if anyone does not stumble in what he says, he is a perfect man, able also to bridle his whole body." (ESV)

The Bible says (and I'm paraphrasing here) that if you can control your tongue, you can control your whole body, and if you can control your tongue, you're perfect. So, just like I learned at a young age the impact that others' words could have on my life, I learned to control my self-talk thanks to Mr. Scothorn believing in me, and I learned to control a horse by taking the reins, so too can we learn to control our tongues.

APPLICATION

Control what you say. Try to say things that are encouraging and when correction is necessary, make sure it is not done out of anger but in love.

Remember sisters, we need to play nice. It's going to happen, you're going to over hear someone saying something negative about you. In that moment you have a choice-- either get all worked up and create more drama, or you can remember that you too have made that same mistake and offer grace.

"Don't eavesdrop on the conversation of others. What if the gossip's about you and you'd rather not hear it?

You've done that a few times, haven't you—said things behind someone's back you wouldn't say to his face?"

Ecclesiastes 7:21-22

Let's make it personal...

We know that not one of us is perfect, so I'm guessing that you've said some things that have made you want to shove your foot in your mouth!

How many times has that happened to you? You say something without even thinking, and it leads to hurt feelings, confusion, conflict, or pain. All because you didn't control your tongue.

How much damage could you avoid if you could learn to control your tongue?

Proverbs 18:21 "Death and life are in the power of the tongue, and those who love it will eat its fruits."

Eph 4:29-32 "Let no corrupting talk come out of your mouths, but only such as is good for building up, as fits the occasion, that it may give grace to those who hear. And do not grieve the Holy Spirit of God, by whom you were sealed for the day of redemption. Let all bitterness and wrath and anger and clamor and slander be put away from you, along with all malice. Be kind to one another, tenderhearted, forgiving one another, as God in Christ forgave you."

Your words can change an atmosphere. They can change the trajectory of a conversation or even the trajectory of someone's life. Mr. Scothorn's positive words completely changed the direction of my life— for the good!

Want your mood to change? Speak positive words or sing a song with an encouraging message (or a worship song).

Want your attitude to change toward someone? Speak highly of them and be kind to them.

Want to encourage others? Don't argue or complain, speak life.

Want to dictate the rest of your day? Speak positively.

Want to protect your marriage? Speak lovingly to your spouse.

Want to raise respectful kids? Speak respectfully and teach them in word and in deed how to respect others as you show them respect.

If you can control your tongue, you can conquer anything. When is it most difficult for you to hold your tongue? Think about that scenario and pray about a game plan to prevent you from lashing out with your words. It could be as simple as walking away.

Be careful little mouth what you say. For your words pave the way, for the life you live and they created your world today. What do you want to go and what you want to stay, all starts with the words you convey.

So be careful little mouth what you say.

Chapter 4

Tracking Stats With SASS

A New Way To Keep Score

When it comes to your relationships, what are you keeping score of?

As the only female in a house full of males, you can be certain that there are certain topics that never get old. In my house there is always food, farting, belching, "that's what she said" jokes, and of course there's the never-ending talk of sports, which includes deep life lessons with the ever-present sports analogies. So, how could I write this book without a sports analogy? This may likely be the only chapter my guys read. So Mutlu Men, this one's for you. It's not that you need it, but I know that you'll read it. (Check it out yo, I'm doing my rap thing. You can't stop this.)

Mutlus and soccer are synonymous. They have a rich history. And by rich history, I mean, my husband grew up playing and still plays every week--up to three times a week. He intends on playing until he is seventy. (It used to by seventy-five but when he hit fifty he lowered it). Anyway, all our boys have played soccer at one point or another. Our older two boys didn't play much after high school and our younger two are still in the throes of it.

Our second to youngest son played on a team that was the runner up for district champs. While there are many games I could talk about, there is one that really stands out. My son's team was playing against another team that had real potential and everyone knew it. The game started off strong on both sides, but quickly turned dirty, both literally and metaphorically! The opposing team had managed to keep our boys from scoring in the first half. It was looking like a clear win for the other side, but then something shifted on the other team, as did the weather. It was like once the rain started coming down hard, it was not only drowning the field, but also seemed to drown out the opponents common sense. One kid made a mistake and then another kid started yelling at him. When I say yelling, I don't mean just a little bit, but a lot. In fact, it wasn't just yelling. If my memory serves me correctly, there was shoving, too. I remember sitting there, nudging my husband, and asking him if he saw what I'd just seen. He sure had.

I'm still not 100% sure about all the rules when it comes to soccer, but I know a few things about the game, and the things I know are what matters for this chapter. For example, one thing I know is that in soccer they keep very few statistics compared to some other sports. There are four areas they track, which conveniently can be summed up with the word SASS.

Scores

Assists

Shots

Saves

1. Scores. Scoring for your team is good. You want your team to get the ball into the other team's net, so naturally this is the best thing to keep score of. This determines who wins the game.

2. Assists. The person who gets the assist is the teammate that passes the ball to the scorer (or the last teammate to touch it before the goal is scored).

3. Shots. Shots on goal, it doesn't even have to go in! Every shot you take on goal, every time you try to score, even if it doesn't work out well and it's a miss, they count the fact that you tried!

4. Saves. On defense there is a record of every time the opponent tries to score a goal and the goal is successfully protected by your goal keeper.

Do you know what they **don't** keep score of? Mistakes. They don't write down in the records what each person does wrong. The record is a reflection of what is done right. Sure, there are mental notes and suggestions from the coach in the middle of the game when a player makes a mistake and does something wrong. The coach will address it, but it's not reflected in the stats.

Of course, that doesn't mean players don't keep track of those stats sometimes. Case in point, let's go back to the soccer field...I noticed that the other team was keeping score, not of the game, but of each other's mistakes. Tempers were flaring, fingers were pointing (and flying), and they lost focus of the stats that mattered. Instead, they were focusing in on things that weren't only not helping win the game, but actually preventing the win and contributing to their loss. In reality, we didn't necessarily win the game that night— but the other team definitely lost the game. All because they had their eyes on the wrong stats.

Once the other team started to break down, our team took off and started scoring. Not because we were all that, but because the other team began to implode. I mean, it was humiliating for them. The rain was pouring hard, the mud was flying, and the other team was cussing each other out. Our guys just kept playing hard and giving it all they had. While our guys made plenty of mistakes, the difference was that they were encouraging one another and not keeping the wrong score. (Just clearing my throat over here!)

Of course it made me think about the stats I track in my own life. For example, how many times in my marriage have I kept the wrong score?

Too many.

My husband won't tell you this (because he's too sweet) but I can be tough. I can sometimes try to correct the way he parents, or even laugh at him when I shouldn't. (Not that you can relate to that, right girl? Haha!)

Another example - How many times have I looked at the my kid's mistakes instead of the shots on goal - AKA what they're getting right?

Too many.

Like when they've cleaned their rooms and instead of looking at the effort they made, and all the things they got right, I see everything that was missed, and I point it out in detail. "Did you not see that piece of paper?" or "You ARE planning on cleaning out under your bed right?" Or, when they come home with a grade letter below what I thought they "should have" received.

How many times have I focused on the bad passes from my co-workers, friends, and family,--the people closest to me?

Too many.

Like when someone says something insensitive and I feel like they should have (Boom! There it is again.) "known better". Or when I needed something and they fell short. I didn't look at all the times they WERE there for me, but instead focused on the one time they missed supporting me.

How many times have I yelled at myself for making big time mistakes in the game of life?

Too many.

Can I tell you that I'm a perfectionist in recovery? I want to keep score of everything that I've done wrong. However, I've had to scale back to the SASS Stats. Because the SASS actually reminds me to stay focused on the positive. In the midst of a game, (life's situations that we face) I can adjust my mistakes and move accordingly, but I'm not taking the record of those mistakes with me. Instead, I'm taking the lessons, what I learned from those mistakes, and carrying those lessons with me to the next match. Those mistakes won't show up in the stats. Those mistakes have been forgiven by Christ, and they are wiped clean permanently from my record.

When life happens and your teammates (your spouse, parents, children, siblings, friends, coworkers and even yes, your pastor) fall short, the LAST thing we want to do is rip them apart because of their mistakes. Yes, in the middle of the game, adjustments and calls will be made, but we can do it with encouragement and love— sometimes tough love.

One of my favorite scriptures teaches me how to treat my teammates and how to love them.

"Love never gives up. Love cares more for others than for self. Love doesn't want what it doesn't have. Love doesn't strut, doesn't have a swelled head, doesn't force itself on others, isn't always "me first," doesn't fly off the handle, <u>doesn't keep score of the sins of others</u>, doesn't revel when others grovel, takes pleasure in the flowering of truth, puts up with anything, trusts God always, always looks for the best, never looks back, but keeps going to the end. Love never dies."

1 Cor 13: 4-8 (MSG)

APPLICATION

Love others with a First Corinthians type of love. Keep track of the right stats. This means keeping track of what they are doing right and holding no record of wrong. Show the same love to others as your Heavenly Father shows you.

Now let's make it personal...

Consider your stat keeping abilities.

Now compare them to the SASS stats by re-reading 1 Corinthians 13:4-8. Are you keeping track of the right stats?

Are there any relationships in your life where you are tracking the correct stats?

What relationship(s) are they?

Are there any relationships in your life where you are tracking the wrong stats?

What relationship(s) are they?

Now I want you to make a list of these people. Instead making a record of their wrongs, I want to take proper stats. Beside each name, write down a record of a right.

If this is a person of significance in your life (like a spouse, child, or someone living with you), I am going to request that you create a special daily journal where you write down something they do right each and every day. By doing this, you can begin to intentionally keep the right stats. Start measuring their SASS!

Score-Write down when they do exactly what was needed or expected.

Assist-Jot down when they set others up for success.

Shots-Make note of awesome attempts at doing what is needed or hoped for, even if they didn't nail it.

Saves-Don't forget to record all the times they defend or protect you or your team. This one can be easy to miss if you aren't looking for it.

Chapter 5

When In Doubt, Kindly Call It Out

Telling The Truth In Love

If you haven't figured it out by now, one thing you'll learn about me as you continue to read through these pages is that I tend to be a little ornery. For example, how many sisters tell their little brother they'll give them twenty bucks to crack three eggs over their head, but instead, only crack two eggs over their unsuspecting sibling's head and then walk away? Well, I know of at least two; my twin and I. Hey, we said we'd give him twenty bucks for three, we never said we'd give him anything for two! My poor little brother, he now uses this example in sermons to talk about how Satan can manipulate us. You're welcome Shawn (and why did I just compare myself to Satan?)!

While being ornery has been a blast, it's also backfired on me a time or two and taught me some valuable lessons. Like this one time when a telemarketer called me, yeah I was having some fun, but learned a major life lesson that I'm about to share with ya.

I remember this one time when I picked up the phone and answered an unexpected telemarketing call. Not wanting to call the guy out, but not exactly wanting to go along with his sales spiel, I decided to take the conversation in a different direction by pretending that I thought that telemarketer was my little brother Shawn pranking me. Sad to say, this just happened a few years ago.

I picked up the phone. We'll call the poor unsuspecting salesman Jim.

Jim: "Hello Mrs Mut-el? Did I say that right? This is Jim with xyz company. How are you today?"

Me: "Why howdy there Jimbo—that was a nice try on the name...It's actually pronounced Moot-Loo. I'm doing Fan-Freaking-Tastic! How are YOU?"

Clearly my energetic and upbeat response caught him off guard.

Jim: "Um, I'm good thank you. I was calling because we were driving in your neighborhood and we saw that you could use some windows. It seems that most windows in your area have been updated but yours."

Me: "Ooooooookaaaaay *JIM*—Really Shawn, I know it's you. But sure I'll bite. Why don't you get me two new sets of windows for the whole house? That way I can save money for the future too— I mean everything is cheaper in bulk right?"

Jim: "Ma'am that's not quite how it works."

Me: "Oh Shawn, the jig is up, I know it's you! You might as well admit it!"

Jim: "Mrs Mutel, I'm not quite sure who Shawn is but I can assure you..."

Me: "OK SHAWN. Good job on continuing to say the name wrong! You got me buddy!"

Jim: "Listen, I have no clue who Shawn is but I can assure you this is NOT him."

NEWSFLASH— I already knew it wasn't Shawn. I was actually hoping the poor fella would think I'd lost my mind and just give up, but he didn't! He kept plugging away, trying to do his job. And here I was, egging him on instead of telling him kindly I wasn't interested. Honestly, I thought it'd be less painful for him to roll with me and move on. BUT JIM WASN'T HAVING IT!

At this point, I was laughing so hard that not only were my eyes tearing up, but so was my bladder!

Me: "Ok, SHAWN, let me just say, I'm not interested in what you're selling, and I sure as heck don't need new windows!"

Reality - I did need new windows. I just didn't want to pay for them. I knew he was a legit salesman, but I really thought it would be a fun story for him to tell his co-workers and for me to tell my friends. If you're out there Jim, I hope you've had a laugh or two at this situation by now!

What I didn't notice during the course of my call with Jim was that my hubby was sitting right there listening to the whole thing. As I was dying of laughter, he was looking at me like I was the cruelest person in the world.

In the end, the life lesson was for me that day. I was reminded that it's always best to be forthright and honest. I wasted poor Jim's time and perhaps even affected his income...Sorry Jim!

Can you relate? Maybe for you it's not a telemarketing call, but if we're honest we can all admit that too often we don't want to confront certain situations because they're, well, awkward. We mistakenly believe that by ignoring these situations, they will miraculously be handled. When instead, the reality is that politely telling someone, "Thank you, but I'm not interested," is a lot less awkward than keeping someone on the phone for twenty minutes making them think you believe it's your brother pranking you. Honesty may be awkward for a brief moment, but in the end it is the right choice.

In retelling this story I'm reminded of Luke 6:31, "Do to others as you would have them do to you."

Would I want someone to do to me what I did to poor Jim, to me? Nope! Would you? Probably not. Although it does make for a funny story, once you've endured the torment! :)

When it doubt, just kindly call it out. Being truthful is best. Even when it might be awkward.

My husband is brilliant when it comes to telling the truth in love. Ladies, I'm sure you can relate to this one. When I put on pants and ask my husband if they make my thighs look big, I want to know the TRUTH! I don't want him telling me what I want to hear. Because then I end up walking around all night thinking I look great, when the fact is, the outfit makes me look worse. Sure, in the moment it might feel good to hear, but it won't serve me well at all in reality. By the way, my husband has an uh-mazing way of answering this question. When I ask the dreaded question, and the answer is, yes, the pants DO make my thighs look big. His response is,

"Well, they make your thighs look bigger than what they actually are." So, he's not telling me I'm fat, he's not telling me I look terrible...he's telling me that there are things that look better! By sharing the truth with me, it helps me. And let's be honest, sometimes I end up changing my clothes a lot because I'm looking for the perfect pants!

Of course, the first thing you've got to do is get honest with yourself and realize the actual size of your thighs. Because it doesn't matter what anyone else thinks, you need to know what the reality is and get truthful with you. Then you're better able to interpret the insight of others. And you can be more confident in sharing the truth (in love of course) with others as well.

APPLICATION

It's better to tell the truth in love--honest and upfront right away. When you're facing a situation that might be uncomfortable to face the truth, remember that being open and honest might be uncomfortable for a minute (or two). However, not being truthful only creates more drama, pain and dread because eventually the truth comes out anyway right? So as one of my gal pals says "suck it up buttercup" and rip the Band-Aid off. Be honest and then you don't have to worry about walking on eggshells all the time. Another plus, you don't have to worry about keeping up a lie. There's nothing better than a clear conscience. Ephesians 4:15-16 tell us that speaking the truth in love, leads to maturity that will help us build one another up. Now that sounds totally worth a couple awkward moments!

Now let's make it personal...

Are there any areas in your life where you've been saying what wanted to be heard instead of what needed to be heard?

Where do you need to get honest with yourself?

Where do you need to get honest with others?

Start first with you. Then once you've built up some confidence and practiced kind honesty with yourself, you can kindly be honest to others.

Would you rather kindly tell the truth and be honest? Or would you rather hold back the truth to spare feelings in the moment, but cause more pain with the lie? (harsh, but needs to be said!)

Would you rather hear truthful words in love or seductive deception?

Chapter 6

PAIN IS NOT THE END

Joy Is On The Way

When you are overwhelmed with pain, it can feel like the end. It feels hopeless. Sometimes it can even feel meaningless. But, that couldn't be further from the truth.

Let me remind you of this spiritual fact. There is purpose to your pain. NOTHING in this life is wasted. None of your pain is in vain...God will use EVERY single ounce for something greater than you can see. You just have to allow Him to do what He wants to do in you.

It was February 13, 2015. I was on staff as the Associate Pastor of a growing church. I had always loved my job there. I loved working with my lead pastor, his wife, the other staff members, and the church body. They were some pretty awesome peeps!

But on February 13th, I was feeling a dread in the pit of my stomach. I was drowning in pressure and I didn't want to go to church. Here's the thing... normally, I'm the exact opposite. I can't wait to get to church and get my praise on! But there was this darkness in the inner part of my spirit that was crippling my zeal and I really did not want to go.

I begged my husband, "Babe why don't you and I take off and drive down to Cincinnati to spend the night for Valentine's Day?" It was like the excuse had been handed to me on a silver platter, and I was delivering it to him, in hopes he would see the shiny object too!

My husband was service director and so he had almost as much responsibility at the church on Sunday mornings as I did. I had already texted my boss and told him I needed Sunday off, so I was chomping at the bit for my honey to agree to an overnight date out of town. I mean, come on, it was Valentine's Day for crying out loud! Surely my husband would say yes!

Nope. Instead he said, "Babe, it's too late. I can't get anyone to fill in for me and so I have to go. I'm really sorry."

I begged, I pleaded, I literally cried out of desperation. I think he thought I was PMSing or something because I normally don't act like that. As devastated as I was, he still said no.

Here's the thing, that date night wasn't about getting out for some quality time with my husband, although it would've been a huge plus. That date was about me getting out of the misery I was sitting in.

I honestly can't remember how long I had felt that way. But I can tell you that I felt stuck under a thumb. I felt like my wings had been clipped and I could not fly. And not because of anyone else... but because I was afraid to pursue the calling God had placed in my heart. It was weird because I wasn't quite sure exactly what that calling was. I just knew I had to start doing something to step into it. Was it writing? Was it doing more counseling? Some life coaching? I wasn't sure. What I did know was it was something other than being comfortable inside the four walls of the church; although, the thought of leaving my job at the church petrified me.

Whatever it was, I had been running from it. Eventually after running for so long I had come to a place where I was miserable.

I remember when my husband told me that he couldn't call off that Sunday morning. I literally sat in my bed and sobbed. I just wanted out. I needed a break. I felt like if I could just get a break, then everything would be ok.

But in reality, no amount of break could release me from the pain I was feeling.

I didn't go to church the next day. My husband and boys went, but I stayed home and slept in. I was stuck in my misery and didn't want to get out of bed. There was no way to outrun the pain. I tried to outsleep the pain, and that didn't work either.

My husband called and said that he and the boys were meeting some friends for lunch after service. These were the kind of friends that knew me as "Holly" not "Pastor Holly," so I was comfortable being around them with swollen eyes and looking like a train wreck. As we sat there waiting on our food, I began to sweat. Heart racing, ears ringing, chest tightening... Was my long lost friend, my buddy the panic attack, coming back for a visit? Or was this in fact a heart attack?

My husband and I quickly left the restaurant and headed for an ER. I knew in my heart of hearts it was only a panic attack. I had been down this road too many times before. All too familiar with this spirit that tormented me... but this time, the torment was something that I had brought on. I was 100% out of the will of God and running from His call. Of course I should have been panicking.

After getting cleared at the ER, and the doctor telling me that I needed to change professions because this was taking its toll on me, (little did she know it wasn't my job that was causing the issue but it was my lack of obedience to God). My husband and I went home and opened up all lines of communication. It had become too easy to keep all my emotions inside and try not to burden anyone else, especially my husband. But he needed to know exactly how I was feeling, what I was going through and the changes that needed to happen in order to get me healthy again. We needed me well.

This pain, at home in my bed, in the moments leading up to the ER, felt like the end.

But in reality, it was just a means...

A means to the end of one stage of my career and to the beginning of what would be one of my most adventurous career moves ever.

Pain was what moved me. I was all too comfortable in the four walls of the church with my happy little life, my comfort zone, and my small little world. But when I kept avoiding the call, I began to feel uncomfortable. I ignored it hoping it would go away. It only worsened. And it was the pain that ultimately pushed me out of my comfort zone.

Just like a Mother Eagle encourages her eaglets out of the nest when it's time for them to fly, so the Lord does with us. He knows that as long as we are warm and comfortable, we won't move. Um, who wants to give up a good and comfortable life, right?

God has had to push me out of the nest on numerous occasions because I'm too stubborn and lazy to go on my own. I've seen myself go through this time and time again. Not wanting to "lose" the battle when in fact it's a step for me to win the war.

Pain gives us the nudge we need to move outside of our normal. It makes us so miserable we'll do anything to try to find a new normal and expand our horizons.

You might even find yourself doing things you'd always said you'd never do. Can I just say, "never say never"? I've learned that lesson all too well.

Living a life of joy doesn't mean your life lacks pain. In fact, the two coexist very well. A life of joy means looking beyond the pain and choosing to allow God to move in the midst of your situation. All you have to do is make the commitment to God and step out into whatever it is that He's calling you to. You decide that that no matter how scary, I mean, exciting (I like to use the word exciting because it sounds more adventurous and fun), you're so desperate you are willing to do whatever it takes to find peace.

And when you do that, you will see that your situation WAS NOT IN VAIN. Your pain was for a purpose. There is purpose in your pain!

Here's what I really need you to know...

You can't have a life of joy if you don't experience pain. Without pain, you don't know the feeling of joy. We must have the contrast in order to know both exist. It's also through our pain that we are more apt to see God moving, because we often sit paralyzed in our pain. In pain, we finally make room for Him to move. Peter tells us to rejoice in our pain, because we will be overJOYed when we see God move through it. (1 Peter 4:12-19)

I think the rapper Rob Base had it right when he talked about Joy and Pain, Sunshine and Rain. I mean they do go together! First, let me just remind you that sunshine and rain, while they frequently occur apart from each other, can occur together at times. When they are both present, we are given the beautiful gift of the rainbow. Just like the sun and rain together allow us to see the beauty of the rainbow, having both joy and pain in our lives allows us to appreciate joy so much more. Big ups (or as the kids these days would say- Props) to my old school dude Rob Base for helping me teach this lesson!

Here's something to keep in mind— even when something doesn't look like it's going to work out, when you understand the joy/pain principle, your faith rises up and tells you that it will be a Romans 8:28 outcome. You also have to remind your feelings that they don't dictate your life, and they don't guide your way. In other words, they aren't your GPS, they are your check engine light. You don't follow your check engine light for directions, you follow your GPS (the Holy Spirit) for directions. Yet, the check engine light lets you know when there is something under the hood that needs to be addressed. The check engine light lets you know that there's pain, but the GPS directs you to the place where the pain is healed. You need both in your life.

Pain is not your final destination. Pain is not the end. It's a means. Eventually it's a means to an end... We are promised that everything works out for our good and His glory! (Rom 8:28) So hold fast to his promise.

APPLICATION

Realize that pain is a natural part of life and embrace it. Trust that God is moving in the midst of your situation, even when it doesn't feel like it. Grab a hold of scripture that speaks to your heart and feeds your faith. Like 1 Peter 4:12-19. It says that we are actually supposed to rejoice in pain so that we may be overjoyed when God reveals His glory in that situation. And boy, does God like to show off sometimes!

Now let's make it personal...

Describe the pain you have been feeling.

Are you being pushed out of the nest? Are you being corrected? How so?

Do you find yourself staying in the nest and fighting for the predictability and comfort of the nest?

Which is greater, the pain of remaining in the same place, or the pain of change?

If you answered the pain of remaining the same, then you are ready to work toward change-- and stepping out into what will bring a sense of joy!

What changes/adjustments need to be made in order to begin to step out in obedience?

Being honest, where do you see God in your pain? If you can't, that's ok...but be on the lookout!

Chapter 7

FIRST WORLD PROBLEMS

Feel The Feels But Don't Get Stuck

I left the mall fighting back tears. Not little tears, but the kind of tears that are like a dam breaking and water flooding through.

Now, I'll admit that it may sound ridiculous and it's totally #FirstWorldProblems (yes I totally just used a hashtag in my book); however, it's my life, and it's legit been a struggle for me.

In April of 2017, we were on vacation and my right foot became really sore and swollen. After six weeks of no relief I finally went to the foot doctor, and found out I had arthritis in my big toe joint— likely a result of wearing high heels and playing kickball (yep, we played in a co-ed kickball league for almost ten years, and I would like to add that I have many championship tee shirts to prove it!). So between both kicking the ball with that right foot and wearing fancy high heeled shoes, it wore away at my cartilage.

My shoe game had ALWAYS been on point. Shoes could make me feel like a million bucks. If I was feeling bad about myself, I'd throw on a pair of heels with jeans and BAM, I was a brand new woman full of confidence.

So there I was. Two foot surgeries later. Two screws, a plate, and a big toe joint that didn't bend anymore. I was in a boot walking through the mall, knowing I was about to purge my entire shoe collection, and to be honest, I was broken inside. It wasn't just about the shoes. It wasn't just that my shoes made me feel more confident. They were also a part of my identity. I know, I know, my identity is in the Lord— but my human, womanly, selfish flesh just wanted her shoes. I was known for having a closet full of killer shoes. And I was going to miss that.

Here's how that day had begun...I was preparing for an evening out, and I needed to have a pair of fancy shoes. The attire was "girl's night out" wear. The only problem was, for me, GNO attire was either a hoodie with yoga pants and Uggs, or an adorable shirt with jeans and my fave heels. The latter was no longer an option. And the former was not possible since the event required dressy attire. The shoes I had in mind were nowhere to be found, and I was in a funk. So my sweet husband, wanting to give me a bit of a pick-me-up, took me out shopping for a pair of fancy flats. And FYI, he has always known that the way to this girl's heart was through handbags and shoes. So, of course he was thinking he was gonna score big!

We hit three or four stores. Nothing. I was so discouraged and he was pushing through and being such the Positive Pat. Finally, we arrived at a store that had some serious potential. My sweet hubby found the most ahhhhdorable rose gold flatforms, which would have been perfect. I got all excited, but there was a problem. You see, my right foot is now wider than my left (thank you surgery) which means there's a whole new challenge to shoe shopping that didn't exist before. Those rose gold flatforms were a no go. What used to be easy and fun was now complicated and just plain sucked. We looked at numerous pairs, I tried a few on and then gave up. I felt so defeated.

Here's the deal.

I had been experiencing tremendous pain, and the fusion for my joint was truly a last resort. The doctor had told me I'd never be able to wear high heels again, but in that consultation, I was in so much pain I didn't care what kind of shoes I'd have to wear, I just wanted to get rid of the pain.

Of course, here we were six months post op and the pain had subsided tremendously. This should have made me so happy, but do you know where my mind went? It went to what I'd lost, not what I'd gained. It was so easy for me to forget about the pain that had caused me to get the surgery in the first place, because I wasn't focusing on what I'd come out of and the healing that had occurred. Instead, I was too busy focusing on what I'd lost - my amazing shoe collection.

As my husband and I walked through the mall heading out to our car, we passed a young man (about my age or even younger) in a wheelchair with a service dog. In that moment the Holy Spirit checked me. I looked at that man and thought to myself, it could be so much worse. I could be in a wheelchair unable to walk. So how about I appreciate the fact that I can walk? How about appreciating the fact that my pain had gone down 90% and that I was so much better than what I was. It was time for me to appreciate what I had instead of what I'd lost.

I admit it, I was grieving. As stupid as it may sound. My relationship with shoes had been beautiful. You see, my weight had always been up and down. But the great thing was that no matter how high or low the number on the scale, my shoe size always remained the same. No matter how much I weighed, I always remained a true shoe size seven-and-a-half. That was constant. When I was down and out, I could go buy some shoes and not have to worry about size. A cute pair of heels, sneakers, platforms, or flats was a great cure all.

And now, my go to retail therapy outlet was over. The reality didn't hit me until that moment when I was standing there at the mall, with the sales girl looking at me like I was crazy.

I'd love to say that I'm all holy all the time and that I fully rely on God 100% and that He is always my go to, and my ev-er-eee-thing. But truth is, shoes had become a small god for me. Writing that out seems so totally ridiculous. I mean, how can freakin' shoes of all things, become such a big deal? Yet, they did become a huge deal in my life. They filled an emotional void. Not only did they fill an emotional void, but they also somehow defined me. People knew me for my cute shoes. Women would always compliment me because I had fantastic shoes. Whether they were super funky, super cute, or super sassy, they were always super! Shoes were a part of who I was and it was time to let that part go.

A few days after that trip to the mall I made the decision to accept where I was at. I knew if I were to keep my old shoes in my closet, they would be a daily reminder of what I didn't have and what I couldn't wear. Keeping them would do nothing to benefit me and I knew it was time to move on. So, I made a public post on social media saying I was selling all my shoes. Do you know I had the most fun selling my shoes? I opened a local Facebook group and posted photos of all my shoes and had an online auction for twenty-four hours. I had so much fun! The ladies were super supportive— all giving their condolences for my loss, while of course appreciating their gain! It was an absolute blast! That gave me the release I needed and then I went and had a blast successfully shopping for brand new shoes!

It's so easy to get stuck on stuff you have to let go of and dwell on what you're missing. But, you need a reminder that the pain is gone. I had to realize that had I not made the decision to fix the pain that had been plaguing me, I still wouldn't be able to wear the shoes I loved, AND I'd be in horrible pain. Maybe you have a similar situation in your life now. Is there something you're holding on to that is keeping you in pain (physical, emotional, spiritual) and you know you need to let go of it? Just like my shoes, it might be hard to let go, but it's worth it to fix the pain. So whatever shoes you have to let go of, I encourage you to embrace a new style. Make a new name for yourself and create a new identity.

Maybe for you it's not shoes. Maybe it's some other physical loss, perhaps it's a church, a relationship, or some other part of your identity. It could be your hair, your youth, that young beauty you once had, or it could be a role you played as a young mom, or the career you once had and now it feels that time has come and gone. And you're grieving. You're in a place now where this change has occurred and you need to recognize that there's no going back. Instead, it's time you appreciate this change for the growth that it has spurred in your life.

And for crying out loud...most importantly, remember what you HAVE and focus in on that! It could always be worse. Someone out there always has it worse. And listen, to be honest with you, I needed to have that moment of sadness. It's OK to feel sad for a season, but you just have to make sure you don't get stuck there.

And at the end of the day, God is moving in your situation...maybe not how you'd like Him to, but how He sees fit. And while we don't always know His ways, we do know that His ways are better than ours, so trust Him. Let go of what you're holding on to and allow Christ to fill the void and be your identity.

APPLICATION

I love that God created our feelings and it's ok to use them all! Deuteronomy 31:8 says, "The righteous cry out, and the Lord hears them...He is close to the brokenhearted and saves those who are crushed in spirit. So sister, accept where you are, feel all the feels. But then make a commitment not to get stuck in your emotions; instead, work through them to continue on from there.

Now let's make it personal...

What is it in your life that has the potential to keep you stuck?

Is there anything that you need to accept to be able to begin to live again?

What is your identity? Who are you? How would you describe yourself?

In what area do you need Christ to redefine you or give you a new identity?

Is there anything in your life that you're allowing to define you that maybe shouldn't?

PACK YOUR BAGS YOU'RE GOING ON A GUILT TRIP

Moved and Motivated by Guilt

I LOVE to dance— I mean, LOVE it! Give me some 80s & 90s hip hop, some 70s club music, or some 2000s boy bands and I'm a dancin' fool!

I don't care what anyone else thinks of my moves...I'm on the dance floor and in my mind, I'm slaying it!

I was raised with lots of "dance lessons," but not your traditional dance lessons. In fact, I'm not talking about any kind of moves you'd find on the dance floor or on a stage. I'm talking about my lifelong dance with guilt. I grew up learning this dance so well that I had perfected it.

Not on purpose. I mean, I don't think so anyway. I don't believe anyone purposely manipulated me into

71

feeling guilty for their personal gain. However, as it turns out, no matter how unintentional, guilt was a big part of my life growing up, and I carried it with me well into adulthood.

My parents divorced when I was seven. After they divorced I lived with my mom until I went off to college so I was about an hour and a half away from my dad. In the sixth grade my mom victoriously battled cancer, and during that time most of my siblings and I lived with my dad. But other than that brief year, I lived with my mom.

So, I guess you could say that my childhood looked nothing like the co-parenting arrangements of today. I got to see my dad once a month and then for extended visits in the summers. When I hit my teen years I was active in the show choir which meant that the visits to my dad became fewer and further between, since show choir was active year round. My less frequent visits to my dad were certainly not on purpose, it was just the demands of school and being a teenager.

Early on after my parent's divorce, I remember being so excited on those weekends when we were going to my dad's place. Then, when my weekend visit was up, there was always this heaviness down in the pit of my stomach— a longing to not have to leave my dad, and feeling guilty when I had to go back to my mom's. There was a heaviness that I felt even as a small child...like having a bag of bricks attached to my back— the load was too big for me to carry, but I picked it up and carried it anyway. When my mom was sick with cancer, and I briefly lived with my dad, I remember feeling that same guilt when I'd leave my mom after spending short visits with her. You can see how I quickly picked up the moves to this guilt dance...it was predictable. When I left one parent, it was a step out on the dancefloor in the darkness.

My feelings of guilt were never about thinking their divorce was my fault. I always, every single time, felt guilty leaving one parent to go to the other parent's house. It's painfully obvious that this was not how God designed family to be.

To add to the difficulty of the situation you need to remember that this all took place back in the day before cell phones, any form of social media, and there was definitely no Facetiming. This was back when we had what was referred to as "long distance" phone calls. For those of you unfamiliar with that term, let me explain...If you were making a call outside of your area code, you had to pay extra for it. This meant that even simple phone calls were few and far between because long distance was super expensive. The lack of communication added more steps to the dance.

You can see where the choreography of guilt was ingrained as a regular part of my childhood. I guess every time I packed a bag to go visit one of my parents, I was not only packing a bag for the visit, but I was also packing for the inevitable guilt trip as well. And with every trip, more dance steps were added.

The intrinsic dance with guilt only grew tighter and more detailed as the years went on.

Though I quickly learned the basic moves of the dance as a child, I continued gaining more experience and learning more intricate steps as the years went on. This dance is something that we get entangled with. It's kind of like being in a mosh pit in the mid 90s—once you're in the midst of it, you gotta fight your way to get out. If you don't, you either keep dancing or it will take you down!

Girl, this guilt thing has jacked us up! It's like we've totally bought into it hook, line, and sinker! Well, at least I know *I* had bought it hook, line, and sinker. I was dancing this dance as if my life depended on it. It became as important as breathing, and yet, in actuality it was suffocating me.

While I lived with this dance for years and years, it was one day, at an old fashioned alter service, that the false guilt, all those lies, and every ounce of shame was shattered. In just one bold prayer, asking God to reveal and remove all the stuff that had kept me bound, the chains of darkness were broken and the once strong, powerful, and dominating paso doble in the darkness of shame and condemnation was no longer. All of a sudden, the darkness turned into light. The dance of guilt became a light, beautiful ballet routine that was choreographed with love and grace. This dance was gentle, free flowing, and unlike any dance I'd ever danced before.

That prayer was a moment of deliverance for me. Through it, I learned the truth, and the truth made me free indeed. It all started with learning the truth, and then by **applying** the truth, I've remained free. It may seem simple, but there's nothing more powerful than prayer. It can release us from all sorts of things, including guilt that has been with us from childhood into adulthood. And girl, if that can happen for me, I know it can happen for you too.

So, let me ask you - Are you free from guilt? I know a lot of people who say they want to be, but they aren't necessarily sure about how to get there. Or, they're so used to having guilt in their life, they don't know how to live without it. It's like it has become part of their identity. No need to raise your hand if that's you, but just know you're not alone and you can do something about it!

So many women I talk to carry around baggage for YEARS. So much so, that they don't know what it's like to live without it. Picture yourself walking, and in your hands are the straps to a bag of bricks that you've been carrying for as long as you can remember. Your hands are calloused and worn. Your body aching, you turn around and begin to walk backwards as you're barely progressing forward. You are tired. You want to give up. But you know you can't.

Someone gently whispers, "release the bag." You're afraid to let go because all you've ever known is holding that bag in your hands. What will you do if you don't have that bag? What is your purpose? Who are you without the bag?

It's time to let go. You build up the courage to finally release it, and all of a sudden a weight has been lifted. You look at your hands and you don't know what to do with them.

And then it hits you— the baggage that you've been carrying has kept your hands full, which prevented you from experiencing so many things. The enemy had you carrying this bag of shame and guilt and he used this bag to keep your hands full. To keep them busy and distracted.

But you've let go. You're now free. Free to fully love others. You can wrap your arms around them and squeeze them with joy! You can freely lift your hands in worship and dance like David danced! Since the baggage has been released, you are able to not only move around, but you are able to do more than you've ever done before, because you aren't weighed down by the baggage. No matter how long you've held onto it, whether it's been one year, or fifty, it's time to let it go. It might feel scary at first, but trust me, it's worth it. Are you ready?

APPLICATION

Take responsibility for your actions, however, realize that while you want to respect others feelings, you do not have the power to control them. And when guilt tries to creep back in, remember John 8:36 if God has set you free, you are free. If you have to repeat that verse over and over again, do it until you can live it.

Let's make it personal...

What baggage have you been hanging on to?

What are the lies that you've believed that caused guilt?

Do you really want to get rid of guilt in your life or have you made yourself comfortable in guilt's company and the attention it brings?

What has kept you holding on to those bags?

Let me remind you dear sister that your past is not a life sentence, it's a life lesson. You gotta quit doing time and start learning the lesson!

WARNING: If you're wanting to continue traveling on your guilt trip and dragging your baggage around, skip the next chapter.

HOWEVER, if you're ready to check your bags for good and be freedom bound, then get out a highlighter and turn the page. We're gonna do this sister!

Chapter 9

BOUND BY GUILT

Bound for Freedom or Bound in Bondage?

There are two types of guilt we experience in life. True Guilt and False Guilt. True guilt makes you bound for freedom, false guilts bounds in bondage. I believe that this is a truth that EVERY person on this earth needs to know.

To this day, guilt still tries to take me for a spin on the dance floor, but like I told you in the last chapter, I have found a way to release that former dance partner and dance with truth instead. Now, when I feel the melody begin to move me and I know the dance is about to begin, I ask myself...am I dancing with the partner of truth and love, or am I dancing with the partner of darkness and shame?

As my grandma used to say, it's time to put your thinking cap on, because I'm going to teach you a little bit here. So get your notebook or highlighter out and start taking notes!

First, I'm going to identify false guilt and what it is. Let me get all pentecostal on ya for a second as I yell at the devil. Get ready Satan you're about to be exposed. And sister, you're about to be set free!

False guilt is what I felt as a kid when navigating my living situation after my parents' divorce. It's that feeling that told me that if I could only just stay at one parent's house, then that parent would be fine, and yet realizing that the other parent wouldn't be. I continuously battled with the idea of allowing myself to enjoy the time spent with either one of my parents, knowing that the other one was hurting while I was away.

False guilt told me as a kid that it was my fault my dad felt bad when I left to go back home to my mom's. As a small child, I bought that lie hook, line, and sinker. And because I bit that bait at such a young age, false guilt became my greatest frenemy.

This feeling of false guilt plagued me in many situations in my adult life as well. For example, if someone wanted me to do them a favor, I would do whatever I could to do it, because heaven forbid I make them feel bad! If I didn't do it, I believed their happiness (or lack thereof) was all my fault. This carried over into every job, every relationship, and everything I ever did. Until the Holy Spirit whispered gently in my ear, "That's not your fault and it's not your responsibility."

Did you know that? Fault and responsibility aren't the same thing. It's not my fault that my parents divorced and that the enemy got in there and twisted it up making me feel guilty when I would leave one parent's house to go to the parent's house. However, it is my responsibility now as an adult to no longer allow false guilt to control me or manipulate me.

I can identify false guilt a million miles away and now I'm going to help you identify it too!

Ultimately, false guilt comes from the enemy. We know that scripture refers to Satan as the accuser and deceiver. He throws around accusations and lies and too often we believe them. When we believe them we begin to feel this false guilt and fall into his trap. He uses this false guilt to make us feel condemned, and never good enough. He wants us to no longer feel worthy. He wants us to forget about our power and authority in Christ. So he seductively whispers lies in your ear.

Things Like:

"If they knew _____ (fill in the blank) about you, they wouldn't love you."

"You're not good enough to do that. Don't you remember what you did and why you carry that shame with you?"

"No one has ever done anything as bad as what you've done. You don't deserve that opportunity."

"Who do you think you are? You've got as many sins as there are grains of sand in the seashore."

False guilt lies to moms and tells them that they can't leave their kids for a girls' night out because it's selfish. It will whisper in their ear that they are terrible moms for wanting to have a little time away.

False guilt tells you that you can't serve in church because of that thing in your past.

False guilt tells you that the reason your spouse cheated on you and left you was because you weren't good enough.

The one thing all of these accusations have in common is shame. When you entertain false guilt, you find yourself dancing in the dark with shame.

Satan wants to keep you stuck in condemnation. He can't have your soul because Jesus already paid the price for that. So now, the enemy adjusts his tactics. His goal is to make you feel so ashamed and unworthy that it paralyzes you from moving forward into the plan God has for you. He wants you to believe his lies to prevent you from living a life of freedom— the freedom only found in Christ. Not only that, if you're stuck in guilt and shame, you won't witness to or encourage others as effectively.

Bottom Line: False guilt holds you back and prevents you from the calling God has for you. False guilt holds you back from a full life in Christ. It binds you up, and it ties you down to everything you used to be. It steals your joy.

I want to shout this from the mountaintops, but since there are no mountains in Ohio, I'm gonna shout it from the pages!

I am here today to remind you my sweet sister (in my best soulful preacher voice) that YOU are a new creation. The moment you asked Christ for forgiveness your sins were forgiven and forgotten as far as the east is from the west. And there is no more condemnation to those who love Jesus...because you are free. (Romans 8:1-2).

You are a daughter of the King.

You are fearfully and wonderfully made.

You are whole.

You are loved.

You are forgiven.

You are new.

You are worthy.

You are the apple of your Heavenly Daddy's eye.

You are the head and not the tail.

You are above and not beneath.

You are loved beyond your wildest imagination.

AND the case the enemy has brought against you has been dismissed by the blood of Jesus Christ!

Rest in that my girl. Rest in knowing that truth.

Funny thing about Satan's lies— no matter where you are in your walk, he's feeding you lies. When you're not walking with Christ, he tells you that you're good enough right where you are. Yet, when you begin to walk with Christ, Satan is always telling you that you'll never be good enough.

Of course false guilt is only one kind of guilt. There's also true guilt. True guilt is the conviction of the Holy Spirit. True guilt doesn't feel good; however, it spurs you into changing your behavior for a holy outcome. True guilt, the conviction of the Holy Spirit, is there to rid your life of the yuck (the sin) and allow more room for Christ to move in your life. True guilt is a spiritual GPS that tells you you've taken a wrong turn. It "reroutes" from right where you are and gives you fresh instructions, with the best route to get to the destination of purpose that God has called you to. True guilt gets you to the place where you are making changes that lead to a life of freedom and growth— a life that is free from sin. When you heed the changes that true guilt is prompting you to make, it prepares you for the plans God has for you. It not only sets you up for what God has, but it helps you walk out your calling and purpose.

When you entertain true guilt, which is that Holy Spirit's conviction, and allow it to lead you, you're dancing with love and grace. Don't get me wrong, the dance ain't always pretty in the beginning...but in the end, the dance is glorious.

So, the next time you're feeling overwhelmed and you're dancing with guilt, look to see who your partner is: false guilt, or true guilt. Are you dancing in the darkness of shame, or in the light of love?

Is today the day that you will release the weight that you've been carrying? The weight that Jesus carried and bore on the cross for you?

As you adjust to your newfound freedom, it's time to learn the dance of truth and love. Filled with grace, the conviction of the Holy Spirit, allowing Him to guide your steps into a life of purpose.

What adjustments and pivots is the Holy Spirit asking you to do in order to be in step with what God has for you?

Are you ready to learn some new moves? Or maybe a whole new dance? You have two choices. You can dance in the dark or you can step into the rhythm of the Holy Spirit.

APPLICATION

Identify whether your guilt is true or false and make corrections accordingly, in order to be freed from its power over you.

False Guilt (Lies of Shame)	True Guilt (Holy Spirit Conviction)
Attacks your character	Addresses your behavior
Painful, shameful & detrimental	Uncomfortable yet beneficial
Tells you that you're not good enough	Tells you that you're better than this
Makes you bitter	Makes you better
Reminds you of your past	Reminds you of your purpose
Paralyzes you and keeps you from your potential	Pushes you toward your calling
Has a negative outcome	Has a positive outcome

The next time you're feeling overwhelmed by guilt, ask yourself if you're feeling false guilt or true guilt with these two questions:

1. Is this guilt preventing you from being the woman God really wants you to be?

2. Or, is this guilt guiding you to positive change so you can walk in freedom to share the love of Christ?

When you answer these questions, you're able to unpack the bags that you've been carrying for far too long and dance freely and confidently into the future...and WITH JOY!!!

Let's make it personal...

Is guilt a struggle for you?

When have you found yourself trapped by false guilt?

Are you currently in a situation where you're feeling guilty? Can you now determine whether it's true or false guilt?

How does this free you up?

If you are experiencing true guilt, take time to deal with the root of the guilt. Pray and ask God for his guidance. Paul tells us in 1 Corinthians 2:10 that Godly sorrow brings repentance that leads to salvation without regret. So be encouraged knowing that treating this guilt won't lead to regret, but it will bring life!

Are you one to use guilt to motivate others? Why do you feel the need to use guilt as a motivator? Most likely you are one who is motivated by guilt. As you free yourself from the guilt in your life, you'll release using guilt to manipulate others as well

Chapter 10

WHEN REJECTION IS A FORM OF PROTECTION

It Ain't Always About You

It was one of our first arguments. To be honest, it was totally my fault. I had dyed our oldest son's hair blonde (His one day Eminem phase. It literally lasted one day and it really wasn't his phase, it was me, lovingly strong-arming him into the look). I had spritzed a spray conditioner on his hair and unbeknownst to me, it had gotten all over the bathroom floor. My husband went into the bathroom, slipped, and almost fell.

This was in the late 90s/early 2000s when the low carb craze had just hit. I was sitting on the couch eating pork rinds when I saw my husband slip. One of my most unlikeable characteristics is that I laugh at the most inappropriate times. I'm one of those people who laughs when someone falls. I laugh when I'm nervous, which means sometimes in the middle of an intense conversation with my husband, I will laugh. I will laugh when my sons are trying to discuss something serious with me and I'm uncomfortable. I've had this issue all my life—I believe it's a coping mechanism from my childhood...and if that's the most dysfunction I have, then I got it pretty good.

Anyway, I digress.

I was sitting there eating my pork rinds when, out of the corner of my eye, I see my husband slip on the bathroom floor. I burst out laughing so hard that I sprayed pork rinds everywhere. He was so upset. I actually hurt his feelings. I didn't mean to. I mean, he knew about my bad habit of laughing. But he was devastated. It was the first time we really got into an argument. He was so upset that he went to bed.

I felt terrible and so I went into the bathroom at 11 p.m. and I mopped up the floor so it was all clean when he got up for work in the morning. I quietly crawled into bed in hopes of not waking him up. As it turns out, he wasn't even sleeping. He couldn't go to bed upset with me (he's so stinking sweet). After a little bit of nudging to get him to open up, he admitted that my laughing really upset him. I tried to explain that I have a horrible habit of laughing at inappropriate times. Here were are, over twenty years later, and I'm still struggling with this laughter thing. He still loves me in spite of it and continues to put up with it. I'm blessed to have a man who loves me unconditionally.

I also know something else about myself. As quick witted as I am and as funny as I can be, that same mouth can lash out when I'm upset. So when we have moments of "intense fellowship" aka, heated discussions, I know that my words can come out strong, and not the way I want them to. This is why I prefer to cool down before continuing a heated conversation. I don't want to say hurtful things. He is my husband, I love him so much, and we are one. My using hurtful words or saying mean comments doesn't do a lick of good. My negative words could cut like a knife and in doing so it could harm our relationship, so I need to take a fifteen minute break (now it's usually only five) to calm down so I can clearly communicate in a way that will not be destructive to him or our relationship.

Do you know that at first he took this time out as rejection? He had been hurt in the past and rejection was a major struggle for him. His temperament is one that needs to feel loved and accepted all the time. And so when I told him I needed fifteen minutes of quiet time, he took it as personal rejection. I had to explain to him that it wasn't rejection, it was actually protection. I was trying to protect him from me doing or saying something ugly and potentially damaging. Upon realizing that it wasn't his issue, this was mine, it completely changed everything.

See, what often happens when we're in relationships is we take things that other people are upset about and we personalize them. We attach the other person's problems to our past hurts and inner dialogue of negativity.

We make it about us, which causes us to perceive their reaction as rejection. Or, sometimes we're hurt by what they do, or we may even believe their response is because of something we did, when in fact it could be that they simply had a bad day.

Often humans internalize someone else's issue. While it is possible that you may have triggered something in the other person, it doesn't always mean you are the problem. Typically, their negative reaction has more to do with something that has nothing to do with you. Maybe you were just the trigger that set it off. (I wanna make sure you're picking up what I'm throwing down--so listen up!) Other people's problems are just that--their problems. So why make it about you? Let them be responsible for their own thoughts, feelings, and actions. You are only responsible for yours. You can only control your attitude and behaviors, you cannot control theirs, so don't take responsibility for them. It's always a good idea to reflect on your own behavior to see if there was something you did. If, after reflection you realize you were in the wrong, then you need to apologize. But my point is that more often than not, the emotional reaction is something much bigger than the situation at hand. In relationships that are meaningful, take time to discuss the situation. Of course, it might be wise to take about fifteen minutes to cool down before talking about it.

Let the other person know that the fifteen minutes you're taking away from the situation is not rejection, it's protection. You're protecting each other from negative, destructive words. Protecting your relationship from further discord and hurt. A few minutes of calming oneself down can save a marriage. You must provide all of your relationships a safe place to share. It doesn't matter if it's a spouse, a sibling, a child, or a parent. When you want to get to the root of the issue, make sure you don't react emotionally, but instead that you respond in love. Truly listen to their feelings. You don't have to agree with them, but you do need to listen and empathize with what they are feeling. This can only happen when the lines of communication are open and not hindered by overwhelming emotion.

The best way to close the topic of conversation is with these two words, "I'm sorry" and then follow up with these next three words, "I love you." Do your best to listen, and then repeat back what you heard them say so you know (and they know) that you truly heard your spouse. Wanna make your spouse feel loved? Make them feel heard. When they know you've heard them and that you want to work together to find a solution, that offers a place of safety and comfort. Everyone needs to feel safe with their spouse. So if you can create that safe space for them, you're creating more opportunity to feel loved, heard, and validated, which will bring the two of you closer together again.

By the way, sometimes other types of rejection aren't a bad thing either. Sometimes, those other things that feel like rejection can also be a form of protection.

It's not just in relationships, it can happen in any area of your life.

That job you didn't get. That speeding ticket that slowed you down. That relationship that ended. The financial disaster that you faced. Getting overlooked for promotion. Those things that at first glance appear to be rejection or a loss, may not be not a setback. They, actually, might be a setup. And usually those setups prepare you for the greatest moments in your life.

I remember in one of my pastoral counseling courses that I took, one of my personal takeaways was that in every difficult situation you face, picture Jesus sitting right there with you. He's watching the whole mess happen, and while you may not understand in the moment why He allows it to play out, later you will understand it. He is sitting there with you, while you're going through it...when you're in pain, He's right there with you to help you get through.

It's so easy to get caught up in the why. Why did this happen to me? Can I tell you sister friend that it didn't happen TO you, it happened FOR you. It's all a part of a greater plan that goes far beyond your mind's comprehension. There is so much more going on behind the scenes, and God is up to something you can't even begin to think or imagine.

A couple of years ago my husband wanted to treat me to a special weekend, so he got us tickets to go see one of my all-time favorite movies that had been turned into a Broadway production—*Dirty Dancing*. NOBODY puts Baby in a corner!

We were so enthralled by all the drama on stage that we missed everything that was going on behind the scenes. We knew there was a lot of action going on behind the curtains and off to the side of the stage, but we couldn't see it because we were so engaged in the show. Every once in a while, when there was a major change in scenes, we would notice that the stagehands were out there doing their thing (we just assumed it was them), because we could see movement. Then, when the next scene began, it was obvious that the production crew had worked their quick miracle to create a whole new scene.

How often in your life do you get so distracted by the drama on the stage of your life that you forget there is a director with a crew working behind the curtain? He's got his crew behind the curtains, off to each side of the stage and He is directing who goes where and what happens next. You can take a minute or two in between scenes to recognize the work He has done, but why not sit in awe and wonder during the show as well?

I remember looking at that production of *Dirty Dancing* and being not only in awe of the spectacular show, but the beautiful scenery props and effects that were created to make for an even better show.

95

If it were just the main characters on stage, the show wouldn't be nearly as good. It takes the director, set designer, lighting department, and a whole bunch of other team members working behind the scenes to create a memorable and spectacular display of artistic creation. And that's what God is doing in your life. Are you giving Him credit for it? Even when you can't see Him, you know He is there.

So, the next time you're in a situation and you can't see all the details as they unfold, or the situation leaves you feeling like you've been rejected in some way, shape, or form, think of the situation like that night at the theater. Understand that there are many things going on behind the scenes, including things you haven't even thought of, or maybe wouldn't understand right here and right now. Trust that God has your best interest in mind, and recognize that the rejection could in fact be a form of protection.

APPLICATION

Sometimes rejection has nothing to do with you. It is more about what is going on inside the other person. So give others the time and space they need. And perhaps when you're going through something it would be wise for you to take some time to step back to be able to clear your mind and get your emotions in check. When you do this, it's best to let those around you know that you're taking time for you, not because of them. And there are those moments when it's just God doing his thing. It may not be rejection, but redirection. So sit back and enjoy the theatrical masterpiece play out as the great Director orchestrates!

Now let's make it personal...

When was the last time you felt rejected?

Was the feeling a result of what the person did or your own personal insecurities?

What would life look like if you were to begin to give people the benefit of the doubt?

What would life look like if you were to begin to let someone else have a bad day and not make it about you?

How great would life be if you just accepted people's answers for what they were and let go of assumptions?

What would your life look like if you quit looking for ulterior motives or what's "really" going on and just accepted a situation for what it is?

How much freer would you be if you didn't make everything about you? And let go of your people pleasing tendencies?

As you find yourself struggling through thoughts of rejection use this prayer to get alone with God so he can help you sort them out.

Psalms 139:23-24

Search me, O God, and know my heart;

test me and know my anxious thoughts.

Point out anything in me that offends you,

and lead me along the path of everlasting life.

Chapter 11

The Glass

Half Full or Half Empty

It was Saturday, January 9th, 1999. A cold and snowy morning. I was on my way to the hospital to give birth to what would be our only daughter. What should've been a ride filled with excitement and anticipation was a quiet and gloomy ride under a gray sky.

Earlier that week, we had two major snowstorms that shut down the highways and buried my car so I couldn't get out. I was supposed to have a prenatal doctor's appointment on Tuesday, but my car was completely inaccessible. So, I rescheduled for Thursday. And don't you know, on Wednesday night a second round of snow came through and buried my car even deeper. I canceled my appointment and rescheduled for later the following week—turns out I wouldn't need that scheduled appointment.

As I lay in bed that Thursday night I was tossing and turning. I just couldn't sleep. My husband who is a light sleeper asked if I was OK. I didn't know what it was, but something had me feeling uneasy. As I rested on my back, staring up at the ceiling, I told my husband, "As soon as I feel her move, I will go to sleep." I laid on my back just waiting for my daughter to roll around, kick, or something. Eventually I fell asleep, but without feeling any movement in my belly.

Friday I got up like every other morning and got around. School had been canceled, so my stepsons were home for the day with me. Like every woman six and a half months pregnant, I was constantly running to relieve myself. But, this time was different. There was something, a small little spot on the toilet paper, and my gut told me to call the doctor.

This wasn't my first pregnancy. You see, I'd miscarried ten months earlier. The baby had stopped growing at six weeks, but my body didn't recognize it. I carried that baby until twelve weeks and then miscarried. Since this was part of my history, my doctors wanted to put my mind at ease. Being that it was a level two snow emergency, they told me to go to the hospital rather than going to my regular doctor's office. Due to the poor road conditions we couldn't get to the hospital my doctors were affiliated with, so instead we had to go to the closest hospital in the area.

I remember the hospital staff taking me back, and I remember changing into that beautiful white and light blue patterned hospital gown (you know I'm kidding, those things are a hot mess!). As I settled into my little area of the emergency room, the nurses and techs came in and wrapped a belt around my big ol' belly, attached the monitor, and began listening for a heartbeat. Of course, at the time I didn't know what they were doing. I just sat there waiting. Soon they began moving the monitor from place to place, waiting for a few moments and then moving it again. After a while, they took me back for an ultrasound. I could see my baby. She was in there all curled up in the fetal position. No words were spoken between the tech and I. I was hoping that she would point out certain features on the ultrasound, like, "Oh look, here's her feet, here's her hands, here's her organs, and her heart". But nothing. Not a word.

I was wheeled back into my small little four walls inside the ER and waited. The hospital was short staffed due to the snowstorm, so it seemed as if everyone was all business and moving quickly.

Then a nurse came in. She looked at me and said, "Honey I'm so sorry but your baby is gone." She began to weep. I sat there numb. I remember her telling me that I would in fact have to go through the process of delivery, and that upon delivery it would be best if I saw my baby, held her, and spent time with her. I sat there void of any emotion. In my mind I was thinking, "Eeew that's so gross, why would I want to hold a dead baby?" It was as if she was talking about some stranger. I was so disconnected from what I was hearing. I was in shock.

As the nurse proceeded to try to convey the words through her tears, my ministerial background came out and I began to encourage her. "I will be ok. I know that the Lord has a plan and I trust Him. He will carry me through this. Everything has a reason."

We were immediately discharged from the hospital. My dad was babysitting our older boys (my stepsons) and we gave them all the news as soon as we got home. I called my doctor and he immediately scheduled me to be induced the next morning.

So there we were on a Saturday morning, driving through the dark cold winter, to be induced into labor so I could deliver my child.

Just a few days earlier all had been normal. I was preparing for a new life to enter this world. As a mom, when you're carrying a child in your womb, you long to feel the movements of your baby, the hiccups that jolt your belly, the kicks, and feeling feet pushing against your rib cage to the point of extreme discomfort.

All that had stopped. When you are carrying a child, you are expecting life, yet I all I could think about was that I was about to give birth to death...obviously, she was living eternally with Jesus in Heaven, but it felt as if I was handed death. The death of a daughter. The death of a dream. And what I didn't know at the time was that this would also be the death of my joy, at least for a while.

I went through a seamless delivery. They doped me up a lot to help me deal with the pain. There were no epidurals, just lots of meds. So to be honest, even looking back now, the delivery itself was like a dream. I can remember parts of the delivery, such as the pain, and my sisters and my husband being there. I remember parts of conversations. And then when the baby arrived, it was like instantly the drugs had worn off and I was awake.

I remember looking at her and feeling so much joy, something like "Honey look what we did, what we created." At the same time I was feeling so much pain and disappointment. A pain so deep I don't have words to describe it.

I have very few pictures of my daughter, but I do have one of the three of us, my husband, my daughter Mia, and myself. You can see the emotional confusion on my face. It was like I wanted to smile because of the child I was holding, but I couldn't because I didn't know if I should be smiling or not. When you give birth to a child that is already gone, is there reason to smile? I remember asking myself what my facial expression should be as the nurse was about to take our picture. I'm not sure that I can describe the look on my husband's face or mine. I can just say I felt both great joy and great emptiness at the same time.

As I sat holding my cold beautiful baby in that stale hospital room, after most of the shock had worn off, I prayed, "God this was not what you were supposed to give me. But I trust you Lord. I know you will somehow work this out for my good and Your glory."

We held a simple graveside service, even with the snow. I remember thinking it was funny how it'd been gray, snowy, and cold since I had found out about Mia's passing in my womb, and yet on that day, the day of her service, the sun beamed down on us— warming my heart and my spirit. Even if just for a moment.

I trusted God. I was raised in church. I knew I served a God that is both loving and sovereign. I knew the words to say, and I knew the scriptures to quote. Both my head and my heart knew the "right" things to say and do, but in reality my heart was also breaking. From a spiritual standpoint, I trusted God 100%. However, my human self needed to grieve.

On the outside I was all smiles, and life went back to normal. By all appearances I was doing well, considering the circumstances. Privately, however, I was struggling. I was trying to see the glass as half full, but it kept coming up as empty.

Soon depression and anxiety gripped me.

In my life I had always tried to see the glass as half full in everything. But now I wondered: Had my glass fallen over and spilled, making a huge mess? Had I lost every drop of water in my cup?

I was gripping on to every ounce of faith I could muster up. I was hanging on to the fact that my glass was indeed half full when it should be shattered, and yet

I still had the desire not just for a full cup, but an overflowing cup...I needed to know that this didn't just happen, but that there was a reason. I had never felt a pain pierce my heart like this throbbing pain. I prayed, please dear God, do not let this pain be wasted... that was the first time I ever prayed that prayer.

Faith is the substance of things hoped for and the evidence of what is not seen (Hebrews 11:1).

I was hoping against hope. This situation was dark and dreary. I was drowning in the deep and I began searching for answers. Some sort of answer, ANY answer good or bad. God just give me SOMETHING.

And there it was. I saw a crystal clear glass. The water went up to about the halfway point of the glass. There is no irony here, considering that during this whole situation I was trying to have a glass half full mentality.

So what we have here is the proverbial question...Is the glass half full or half empty?

It is human nature to base our assumptions off of what we see. Some people see it as half full. Others half empty.

You and I both started off our lives with a glass that was totally full of water. Over the years, life hit some bumps and some of the water was knocked out. Those hard times drain you. Unhealthy family dynamics, divorce, financial struggles, sickness or disease, relationships that let you down...So much loss starts to build up that it feels like your cup has a leak. It doesn't, it's just that all the unexpected turbulence in your life caused your cup to spill.

Then there are people who come into your life who drink from your glass of water. Perhaps they made it appear that they were taking a sip when in fact they depleted a lot of your water. Maybe they intended on refilling it when they were done, but they didn't know how, or where to find the water to help fill it back up. These types of relationships can take a toll on your joy.

I'm guessing that you my sweet sister have been through some things that have caused you to look at your glass with a critical eye.

But, let me ask you this - Do you see it half full or half empty?

When you're trying to make sense of your pain, it's easy to see the glass as empty, even when we desperately want to see it as half full. That's where I was at when I was trying to make sense of all my pain.

And then, I had a thought. What if we didn't base our assumptions off of what we see or how we felt, but instead we came to a conclusion based upon what God sees and what He promises?

As I stared at that glass with water in it I wondered, how can I start to see this glass as half full?

The answer finally hit me. The cup wasn't half full. It also wasn't half empty.

The message God was downloading in my spirit was more clear than that glass in front of me. It didn't matter how much friggin water was in there. The glass was actually 100% full. Not half full as it appeared, but filled to the brim. And dare I say, it was even overflowing!

What do I mean? Well, at the time I was only looking at what I could see— the water. And, I believed that the water was the only thing that could fill the glass. The water was what I wanted, it was what I thought I needed, and therefore it was where I kept my focus.

Call me crazy, but it doesn't matter what we actually *see* in the glass. It doesn't matter what it looks like from our human angle. When you take a look and see the glass from a supernatural angle, or, in other words, from God's perspective, you will see...

That yes, half of the glass is filled with water, but what we don't see is that the rest of it is filled with air. And yes, that air is overflowing!

The WHOLE glass is full!

It may not be something we can see or want to see at the time, but eventually when we look hard enough, when we begin to pray to see things in a different light, if we are open to fresh revelation, we can see that our glass is totally full. It may not be what we wanted in the glass. I mean, when I'm thirsty I want a whole cup of water with extra ice (can I get a witness?). However, God in His sovereignty sees that I might want a whole cup of water, but I only need half the glass...and sometimes

107

even less. Because I need more of Him. And the more water that's in the glass, the less room there is for Him in my life!

If He is the air that I breathe (and that's my prayer, that I'm constantly breathing in more of Him), why wouldn't I be grateful for the air in my glass?

When my glass is totally full of what I think I want and need, there's no room for the air. However, when the glass is emptied of me, there is room for Him. So often in my life, I have neglected to search for Him. I'm not saying I'll always see Him moving, but I don't need to see Him to know that He is there. I know He's promised me He will always be there, and we have to hold on to that promise.

So in those moments where it feels like you're totally empty and reduced to nothing, that's when God can do His greatest work.

We only see in part. God sees in whole.

I can only see the water. Yet when my faith is activated, I realize it doesn't matter what I see, it's what I know to be true.

When this realization hit me, everything changed.

My daughter, while she NEVER took a breath outside my womb, had served a purpose. Her life has touched MANY lives— including many that I may never know about. It was losing her that led me down the path to helping others struggling with anxiety and depression. God knew just what I needed and He filled my glass even when I didn't know it. My glass had, and still has, everything I need.

I don't need a cup full of water. I want a cup full of what God knows I need. When I know Him to be true, when I know His promises to be true, it doesn't matter how much is in my cup, I'm grateful He saw fit to give me one!

What is your situation today? Do you see a glass half full of water? Do you see it half empty? Or, can you look through supernatural eyes to see what God sees? That the entire glass is full, even if it's part air. He knows what's in the other half of your cup even when you don't.

Perhaps it's time for you to think outside of the box, or outside of the glass if you will. Look at it from your angle and then look from the supernatural angle. You may not see it, but I encourage you, even when you can't see it or detect it, to trust that it's there. Begin to pray to see things from a supernatural standpoint and not just with your flesh. The flesh will tell you the glass is half empty. The Spirit will tell you the glass is 100% full. You may not know all the answers, but you can have faith, knowing that the glass is full and that God's got a purpose for it all...even when it may have fallen over and spilled water all over the place...the glass is STILL full. You just can't see it. That's when faith rises up and we choose to trust God.

If you want a life full of joy, you can't stay focused on what you don't have or what's missing. Yes, you grieve. You have to go through the human process of grieving, but the point is not to get stuck there. You must recognize the loss but also begin to live again. And when you choose to live, you choose a life of joy and being grateful for your blessings instead of being bitter for your losses.

YOU HAVE THE CHOICE—You've got one life to live here on this earth—you've got one cup to give—GIVE IT YOUR ALL!

APPLICATION

Shift your perspective from your eyes to the eyes of God. When you do this, your situation might not change but the way you see it does. And when you're looking through the eyes of God, you are able to see beyond your feelings and into His greater purpose.

Now let's make it personal…

What areas of your life have you been looking for what is missing rather than what is there?

Would you rather sit in the misery of what you don't have or the blessings of what you do have?

Make a list of every blessing you have. Which blessings surprise you the most? Which blessings started out not as blessings but as painful packages? Would you do it again-- go through the pain to get to this place of gain?

If you're looking at your list and still seeing nothing but lack, look at the list again and again until you're able to see it through the eyes of contentment. Perhaps a visit to a homeless shelter, a prison, an unhappy home or a missions trip is in order.

Things aren't always the way they appear. Sometimes the poorest people are actually the richest.

What makes you the richest person you know?

Chapter 12

The Power Of The Prank

Releasing Laughter In Your Life

I was in a very dark place after my husband and I lost our stillborn daughter Mia. I was clearly struggling with some serious anxiety and depression. After trying to "fix it" myself for about ten months, I finally went to the doctor and started counseling.

I remember during one of my first counseling sessions my counselor said, "You need to get your joy back." Well, duh, I thought. I'm anxious, depressed, and overwhelmed. You think I might need my joy?

When you're in that state, it's very easy for sarcasm to make its way to the surface about as quickly as a bubble in a pot of boiling water.

She recommended I play a simple prank on my husband in order to start finding joy in my life, and we decided I would short sheet our bed. Just in case you're

113

unfamiliar with the old short sheet technique, here's how it goes...You take the top sheet and fold it in half, tucking the bottom half under the top of the bed (disguising it as the fitted sheet) and then, when you go to crawl in bed, your feet get stopped. Back in the day, it was a good joke. Nowadays, it's quite lame. However, it's harmless, and no one gets injured, or at least it's not likely.

So, I short sheeted the bed. I'm not sure that we really laughed that hard. But it stirred something in me that allowed me to have fun around the house again. Next, I started de-pantsing my husband again. There's something about him standing at the kitchen sink doing dishes in his athletic shorts that just begs to be de-pantsed. I want to clarify, I only pull down his athletic shorts so he is still wearing his undies. His hands are wet, usually covered in dish soap, so he's helpless in pulling his pants back up. That's still one of my favorite go to pranks.

Then there's the old wrap the rubber band around the kitchen sprayer one. This one always catches the unsuspecting person off guard. When they go to turn on the kitchen faucet the sprayer is automatically on, and the individual gets sprayed nonstop.

That counseling session clearly was worth every penny. My family is still getting great joy from playing pranks today.

Although, sometimes the pranks go a little too far.

With the permission of my husband and my son, I want to share with you the one prank that goes down in the Mutlu Pranks Hall of Fame. Not everyone thought it was funny. However, everyone but the victim was rolling in laughter. It took a little time, but now even the victim will smile as we recount every sordid detail of this classic.

Before I go any further, let's do our due diligence.

Warning: Do not try this at home. The described prank below was done by professionals with supervision and extreme caution. This one is not for the faint at heart.

OK, so my third son is the king of all pranks. One day he decided to grab an assortment of sauce packets from Taco Bell: mild, hot, and verde in order to create the ultimate prank setup. Here's what this clever guy did: He took each packet and slightly twisted it in the center to create the perfect level of pressure. With just the right amount of squeeze, well, I'm sure you've figured out what might happen. If you haven't, you soon will.

Knowing my husband would soon be off to the restroom, my son placed a twisted packet of Taco Bell sauce under the different pressure points of the toilet seat. In case you're wondering, these pressure points are the lines on the toilet seat that keep it lifted just above the bowl itself, and create a space between the toilet bowl and the seat. My boy's ingenuity was fast at work. He placed a twisted packet of sauce under each line to create massive pressure when the target would sit down on the toilet. That day's target was none other than his dad (my husband).

What makes this story even better was the fact that we had witnesses. My sister, who was living out of town at the time, happened to be visiting for the weekend. My son warned her, "This is gonna really make my dad mad, but watch, it's totally going to be worth it!"

Of course the moment of truth arrived. My husband innocently worked his way into the bathroom. He dropped his drawers, and as he sat down he saw something shoot onto his underwear. Pretty soon it was dripping down his legs. And it began to burn.

At this point, my husband was in full blown shock and came shuffling out of the bathroom, white as a ghost. Boxers and shorts around his ankles, shirt drooping down just enough to prevent exposure, and a look of sheer panic on his face as he waddled like a duck out to where we were waiting.

He saw us ROLLING in laughter, and right away he realized what was going on. But here's what makes this prank even funnier—our son had pulled this prank once before. The first time, I laughed so hard I fell off the couch, and while his dad was mad at first, eventually he started busting a gut too. But this time was different. This time there were no signs of laughter.

My hubby pulled up his extra saucy pants as he felt the burn, both physically and emotionally. He was furious. His first order of business was to send our boy to his room for the night. In the meantime, my sister and I were laughing so hard that it became a silent laugh...Nothing coming out of our mouths but our bodies shaking because we were still rolling. At this point I knew my hubby was mad, so I had to hide my laughter. This meant we pulled blankets over our heads, and while there was no noise, my husband could see we were still shaking.

Here's the thing...I knew I was upsetting him with my laughter. Of course you know how much he loves that nervous laugh of mine. At this point in the prank, my laughter shifted from the hilarious prank laugh to that nervous laughter. I tried to pull myself together, but I had tears dripping down my face. I was wearing a perma-grin, yet trying to pull myself together to look concerned and tell my hubby I was sorry. I was not successful.

My husband furiously went upstairs to our room to change, while the rest of the household departed into their beds for the night. The whole prank went a bit too far.

Although we had all retired for the night, the laughter still continued. My sister text me a pic of herself, in the guest bedroom, still laughing. Of course, this prompted my laughter to try to make another appearance, but I fought it back with a cough. My poor hubby was rightfully frustrated with me for laughing at a joke that our son had been told not to repeat, so I had to keep a straight face. I also apologized profusely.

After the apology, telling him that I love him, and after admitting I shouldn't have laughed, all was finally well.

In fact, my husband eventually lightened up and actually began to chuckle himself. My son apologized for pulling a prank he was told not to pull again. As for my sister, well, she's still laughing about it.

While humor is a go-to stress reliever for the Mutlus, the fact of the matter is, we all need something to give us a good ole fashioned belly laugh every once in a while. I get it, you're busy. You get so caught up in the day-to-day stress of life. With your to-do-lists, bills, worries, having to live up to all these expectations both from others and ones you put on yourself. It's no wonder that sometimes you need to just throw all that out the window and make some room for fun. Laugh a little. Obviously you don't want to be cruel and I know we set a horrible example for you with the taco sauce. Clearly that prank is dangerous on several levels, but the lesson to be learned in all this is that it is so important to laugh and live joyfully. Even when it feels like all hope is lost, or that you can't get your joy back, if you try, you'll find that it can be done. And hey, if you're looking for a way to add a little joy to your life, you might consider some silly HARMLESS pranks to start bringing back that fun.

APPLICATION

Is it time to start adding some spunk and silly sauce back into your life?

What are some HARMLESS pranks you can do on your loved ones? Here are a few of my faves:

- Moms with littles, when dad gets home, everyone lay on the floor and pretend like you're sleeping.
- Put extra salt in cookies
- Put toothpaste in Oreos
- Pull the old "I'll give ya $20 to crack three eggs over your head" prank! (Refer to chapter five if you need a refresher.)
- Stuff the tips of shoes with toilet paper/paper towels/Kleenexes
- Whoopie cushion
- Fart machine (I'm requesting this be done at my funeral when people walk by my casket)
- Fake Spiders/Snakes—always a fun one!
- Fake lotto ticket
- Dip an onion in caramel to make it look like a caramel apple
- Put Skittles, M&M's and Reese's Pieces all in the same bowl.
- Fill a room with balloons
- Wall/car covered in post it notes

- Cover the floor in Solo cups half filled with water.
- Short sheet the bed.
- When out to dinner, and a guest goes to the restroom, hide their plate when they come back.

Make your list of silly pranks or fun that you can begin to implement into your life.

Now let's make it personal…

How much laughter lives in your home?

Take a moment to ponder, is it even welcome? Are there any unspoken rules of when it is or isn't appropriate?

Ask your family members, is humor, laughter, or pranks encouraged?

How would life change if you were to add a few harmless pranks here and there?

Perhaps pranks aren't your thing, that's ok. What about jokes? Can you share jokes, funny stories, or get creative with your own flare?

After implementing laughter in your home for some time, do you notice a positive difference in the dynamics of your family?

Look at what scripture tells us. As we laugh together, God gets recognized.

"Our mouths were filled with laughter, our tongues with songs of joy. Then it was said among the nations, 'The Lord has done great things for them.'" Psalm 126:2

Chapter 13

Burning Embers: Part One

Walking When It Hurts

When I was a kid we lived on a tobacco farm. We had some cows, and if my memory serves correctly, some chickens too. And let's not forget the farm cats that kept the mice situation under control. When you're a child that lives out in the country, the world is yours to explore. You're outside running around with no shoes on, and the worst possible injury in mind is getting stung by stepping on a bee in the clover filled grass. Playing in the outdoors always meant endless possibilities of entertainment and fun. Life was so simple back then. Water was always freshly flowing from the outdoor faucet, so when you'd played up a sweat, you grabbed a swig of water from the hose to quench your thirst.

One of my favorite things to do on hot summer days was to pop the hot tar bubbles in the middle of the road. Before you freak out and panic because my parents let me play in the middle of the road, let me tell you that there were about five cars (ten max) a day that would drive on our road and typically it was only the neighbors (who had kids who enjoyed popping tar bubbles too so they knew to watch for us). Of course this was the early-mid seventies when kids were actually encouraged to play in the streets!

One of my earliest memories, that is still vivid in my mind, was chasing the cat around the yard with my twin sister, Heidi. My dad was working in the barn, and my mom, who was pregnant with my younger brother, was at the doctor for a prenatal checkup. I had no clue where my older brother and sister were because I was having too much fun with Heidi chasing the calico cat. We ran playfully through the green grass in our bare feet, giggling along the way. The cat was first, Heidi was second, and I followed behind. It seemed like just an ordinary day, but things were about to take a turn. The cat crossed over the gravel driveway and we continued to chase it. We had played so much outside that our little feet had grown somewhat callused to the gravel. Plus, we had learned how to run across it really fast in a way that made it so it didn't hurt too bad, at least not bad enough to prevent us from running on it. So, the cat crossed over to the other side of the gravel, close to the field, and just as quickly as the cat crossed the stones, so did we.

What I didn't know was that on the other side of the gravel was a fire. My eyes were looking for the cat, not for danger.

It wasn't a big, fancy, flaming fire. This fire had been burning for a few days, so the outside was covered with various shades of black, white, and gray ash. Lurking beneath the ash were bright reddish orange glowing embers. These embers were just as hot beneath the ash as the original massive fire that had burned days prior. They were, in fact, hot enough to reignite a fire.

The cat lightly ran, almost as if it were floating, over the light gray coals and crossed the ash with ease. Heidi ran around the fire in hopes of cutting the cat off on the other side. Me on the other hand, well, I was still playing Simon Says with the cat, and clearly Simon had said to cross the fire, so I did. However, the weight of my toddler body was enough to sink through the light gray ash down into the burning embers. It was as if my feet melted into the bright colored embers. And my memory leaves me there...

What's left are a few vivid pictures in my mind, like clips of what happened next. Almost like movie trailers.

I remember my dad picking me up, running me into the house, setting me on the white formica countertop in the bathroom with my feet dangling in the sink. He was holding my feet under the cold water, trying to soothe them as I screamed bloody murder in pain. Each foot was like one big blister.

The next thing I remember was being at the hospital, in what I now know as a crib, with bars up the side. I remember my grandparents bringing me a black and white teddy bear that was bigger than me...I loved seeing that bear in bed with me.

What I didn't love was the fact that my feet were extremely tender. I remember the nurse coming in the room, the white dress, white panty hose, with white shoes, and a weird shaped white cap on her head. I felt like she was so mean, why wouldn't she just leave my feet alone? Those nurses were always coming in and messing with my feet, and I didn't know it at the time, but the feeling that I felt when I saw them was dread. My feet were bandaged and throbbing, yet this nurse would come in and she would change the soaked bandages. I would look down at my feet and they were just massive blisters. I wanted them to leave me alone, but they wouldn't. As an adult, I now know that they had to change the bandages, no matter how painful. They were doing everything they could to prevent infection and to ensure that my feet would heal properly.

I remember knowing that I didn't want to walk at all. I just wanted to lay down and sit. But at some point, the doctors told the nurses that I needed to start walking. So, those nurses would make me walk on my painful and bandaged feet, regardless of how much pain I was in. I kept thinking, if this woman was supposed to help me, why was she making me hurt so much? I honestly felt like she didn't care about how I was feeling.

I can remember crying as she took my hands and I slowly took each step. My mind couldn't grasp the concept that in order to heal properly, I'd have to push through pain and discomfort. That yes, it was going to hurt at first, but if I didn't move, I would be worse off. This was a necessary part of the healing process.

My nurse had committed to my long-term healing, regardless of my short term pain.

Healing doesn't always feel good in the beginning, does it? In fact, the beginning of healing is usually when it's most painful. But when the plan is set before you, and the decision and commitment are made, that's when the healing process can begin. While there is a guideline for healing, it's not necessarily a guarantee. There are lots of factors that go into how long healing can take, and there are different things that can go wrong. Every situation is unique. And yet every situation starts with the decision to get help to heal.

While I wasn't old enough to understand it at the time, the people who were entrusted to care for me knew better. Regardless of my screaming, my temper tantrums, my feelings, and my whining, they had committed to seeing me get well. They knew better than I did about what I needed, and since my parents trusted their wisdom and knowledge, I found healing.

Today, not only do I have the memories of that awful burn, but I also have the scars. When I look at the scars I am reminded that I can make it through anything.

Whether a physical burn like that fateful day with the fire, or an emotional burn, I can do this. Little did I know that it would be that physical burn that would encourage me to heal from an intense relational burn I would encounter in my adult years. One like no other in my lifetime.

APPLICATION

After a painful experience, rest when you need to, but don't get stuck there. Get up, walk, and when it's time, continue on with life (whatever that looks like in your situation). Psalm 41:3 says, "The Lord nurses them when they are sick and restores them to health." You aren't in this alone, your Healer is right there with you and He won't leave.

Let's make it personal...

Has there ever been a time when you've been burned?

Did you find yourself staying down and playing it safe to prevent more pain? What is it that kept you down?

Did you rest when needed and get up and get moving? What was it that inspired you to get up and walk through the pain?

How did you (or how can you) grow from your pain?

Chapter 14

Burning Embers: Part Two

Forgiveness Is Not A Feeling, It Is A Commitment

When I forgive someone I want to just let it go. Be done with it. End of story. Period. #NoGoingBack. Yep another hashtag! (in my rapper voice) You Can't Stop This!

I don't like icky feelings.

I don't like that bitterness that rises up and makes my insides feel so dirty that I have the urgency to shower.

While forgiveness does get rid of bitterness, it's not an instant stain remover for icky feelings.

You said my name wrong and you're sorry? Gurrrl, no problem, no worries. It's forgiven and already forgotten. Boom. Let's move on.

I'm not talking about the, "You let me go through that entire dinner party with lipstick on my tooth?" type of forgiveness here either.

Let's get deep sister. I'm talking about the kind of forgiveness required when someone you love ripped out your heart, stepped on it, then put it back. You tried to forgive and then they busted open your chest, grabbed your heart again, stepped on it, took a bite out of it, and then spit it out. Yeah, that type of forgiveness is HARD.

It's the kind of forgiveness that comes from a situation that makes you want to throw up every time you think of that "thing" that hurt you. Your insides are wanting to cuss you out for allowing them to feel that kind of pain, and you want to run from it or somehow fix it, but you can't find a way to get a resolution. But right now, there isn't any other option...Except forgiveness. Not the easy, it's done forgiveness, but the long drawn out process of forgiveness.

Here's where it gets tricky...while you know the very thing you need to do is forgive, you don't want to do it because you know you've been wronged. It feels like if you decide to forgive, then what you're really doing is letting them off the hook. Or worse. You might feel like forgiving means that you're pain is forgotten.

So many people think that forgiveness is a feeling that is felt, when in fact it is a commitment that is made. And the first step of that commitment is making the *decision* to forgive. Sometimes it's a decision that's made over and over again, on the same offense, with the same person. We commit to the decision to forgive, and eventually, healing takes place and the feeling of relief will follow.

The Bible says in Matthew 18:22 to forgive a man seventy times seven times a day and let's be honest, sometimes it takes that many times to forgive just one sin. Just when we think we've forgiven it, those ugly feelings suddenly begin to rear their ugly head again and we have to remind ourselves that we made a decision to forgive REGARDLESS of our feelings.

I had a situation once that demanded this type of forgiveness with a very dear friend. When it comes to the hierarchy of my friendships, my husband is my ultimate best friend. Next, there are my sisters— they are there no matter what. My husband and my sisters are my ride or dies. Then there are those friends that are so few and far between, they are the kindred spirits. They are like a sister, but literally from a different mister (and Mrs.). Not blood, but framily— friends that we choose to make family. Someone that you can communicate a whole sentence to with no words, just a look.

This type of friend is one of the first people you want to call when you get great news. She's also first on your list to dial when something is wrong. Have you ever experienced this? You call your friend, who doesn't know a thing about the situation you're going through, but as soon as you hear her voice say "hello" on the other end of the line you feel so safe that your voice cracks and you break down before the conversation even begins. The shortest way to explain a sistership like this is just to say that she feels like home.

I had her. She was my person. Yet, I'm not sure where it actually went wrong. I was making some drastic changes in my life, changes directed by God, and I knew I had to be obedient. These were major, life altering, course correcting pivots for me that were part of God releasing me into my purpose. Those changes weren't easy for my husband and I, let alone those who didn't understand what was going on, or those who thought we were making a mistake.

I can only imagine the pain that she must have felt, as well as the sense of loss she experienced as a result of my changes. However, we committed to making our friendship work no matter what. Little did we know we wouldn't be able to beat the "whats" that came up.

Here's the strange thing — I can't even tell you one specific thing that happened.

Looking back on the situation, I think it's safe to assume we both hurt each other and to be honest, I don't even remember the timeline. It's all one big blur. We would say we were going to make our friendship work, and then something would happen and I wouldn't hear from her. Eventually one of us would reach out, and we'd be back on track for a month or two, but then it would happen again and we'd lose track of each other.

After happening so many times, one time eventually became the last time.

The episode I remember was that she was supposed to call me one week, and then weeks turned into months, and then months turned into a couple of years. After two years, with no response to my texts, the realization hit me...I had been ghosted, and with no explanation as to what I had done. Clearly something had happened, I just happened to be left out of the details.

I felt burned. Not an "I accidentally touched the stove" kind of burn where you quickly react and jerk your arm away from the source of heat.

No, this was more of a sunken into the depths of the heat, unable to get out on my own type of burn. Just like when I was child trying to run through those burning embers and my dad had to pull me out.

Have you ever experienced that type of burn?

I can honestly say that the emotional burn I experienced when my friendship went up in flames was the to equivalent in pain that physical burn I experienced in my childhood.

So there I was, grieving the unexplained loss of my best friend, and wanting to process this grief with her. But it just wasn't possible. She wasn't there for me. I knew there was only one person I could reach out to that would help walk me through this— the Holy Spirit. I knew the Holy Spirit would walk me through this painful time just like my nurse walked me through my healing as a little child.

And I was desperate for healing.

One Sunday morning during service, I remember being on the platform in the middle of leading worship, and I began to pray. I told the Lord, "God I know who you are, I know you love me and you want what's best for me. And in that, there are times when things change. I know that you give and you take away. This situation sucks and I hate it but no matter what I'm feeling right now, I choose to trust you. I know you will see me through. You are what I need. God I'm crawling up on your lap and need you more now than ever."

It was then that I saw an image that explained it all.

In my mind's eye I saw me standing with crutches that were actually holding me up. I realized I had become so dependent on those gray crutches that I felt I couldn't walk without them. Then, out of nowhere, the crutches were knocked out from under me, and I was still standing. I began walking, not with the help of the crutches, but with the help of God.

At that moment I realized that I had been depending on my best friend for so much. I'd been depending on her more than I was depending on God. Now, I'm not saying that God ruined our friendship so that I would lean on Him more (although He clearly allowed it to happen). What I am saying is that through losing that friendship, I knew that the ONLY person I could ever depend on wholeheartedly, that would not let me down, was my heavenly Father.

I had been burned so bad from that relationship. I had to trust the Holy Spirit to walk me through the process of healing, even when it was so painful I wasn't sure I was going to make it. I depended on Him for every step I took.

I made a decision to forgive and committed to it so that I could get rid of all the emotional infection that I was carrying around. There were many times that I had to remind myself that I had forgiven her. Even though it didn't feel like I had. I had made a commitment to do so.

Eventually, after remaining true and honoring that commitment, healing took place. It wasn't overnight. In fact it took a long time, but eventually I healed. How do I know? You know you're fully, 100% healed when you no longer feel that icky feeling you once felt when you think of that person or situation.

By the way, forgiveness is not condoning the offense. Forgiveness isn't always forgetting what happened. Forgiveness isn't letting the offender off the hook. Forgiveness doesn't even have to involve the other party.

Forgiveness is simply making a decision to no longer give the offense and the offender power over your life. It is writing off a debt that can never be repaid. Unforgiveness and bitterness keep you attached to the offense and the pain. They hold you captive.

Picture yourself inside a prison. You're in the prison, and in your hand you hold the key that unlocks the prison door. Yet, you won't unlock it because you believe the offender needs to "do their time" and "pay" for what they did, but here's the thing, harboring unforgiveness does not imprison the offender. It actually imprisons you.

I remember preaching a sermon once about the power of forgiveness. I shared how we might have the "right" to feel angry and bitter, but asked whether allowing ourselves to continue to feel that way was helping or hurting? Afterwards, a mom came up to me bawling. Her daughter had been sexually abused. The mother did not want to forgive the man that had hurt her daughter. However, she realized that forgiveness didn't mean she was condoning his horrific behavior. It actually meant it would no longer give his horrendous assault power over their lives. It was forgiveness that would release them from the assailant.

When you don't forgive, whether it's conscious or not, you are choosing to keep yourself connected and attached to the very thing that caused you pain to begin with. By holding onto the pain and not forgiving, you are willingly carrying that heaviness that the offender and situation brings. It's like imprisoning yourself in a torture chamber while you hold the key. You're forcing yourself to relive the same painful situation over and over again, keeping yourself in agony. Since you refuse to forgive, you're inflicting that torture upon yourself. And likely, you're blaming the other person for the torture you've endured due to your unforgiveness.

YOU HOLD THE KEY! You have the power and the authority to release the torture by forgiving. When you choose to forgive, you cut the weight that has been holding you back. You may not feel the release of the weight right away, but eventually you will.

Flash back to my friend... I had committed to forgiving her. I just had to remind myself over and over again that it was done and it had no more power over me. As I did that, the ugly feelings began to dissipate. I just had to continue to remind myself of my commitment to forgive.

In all honesty, as I prepared to write this chapter, I faced a lot of pain. As much as I didn't want to get burned by the fire again, I approached it. This time with a whole new respect for the flames. Both the obvious flames and the embers lurking beneath the surface.

I messaged my old friend because I didn't want her to be caught off guard by this chapter (just in case she ever read the book). We ended up getting together for breakfast the same week I got in touch with her. When I saw her, there was no awkwardness, no pain, and no anger. There was just a deep compassion coming from both sides.

The conversation began lightly and we asked each other about our families. We didn't rehash ugly, painful details from the past, but instead there was a lot of mutual understanding. The same type of understanding that we'd always had. We knew each other's pain, we knew each other's regrets, and we were able to identify where the enemy had whispered lies in our ears, and we realized that we had believed them.

As we sat there, both of us had tears in our eyes, and we wondered why it took so long for us to reconnect. I reminded her that God wastes nothing. I vocalized my desire to share our story. I would not let our pain be wasted, knowing that there are so many women who struggle with the pain of losing friendships and living in isolation for so long.

I'm not the only one who has gone through this, and neither are you. Today I tell you my sweet sister, you are not alone. There are countless homes filled with empty sisters, sitting in solitude, believing that they are the only ones feeling this way. Your mind gets seduced into thinking that you are the only one who has ever been left out in the cold and hurt this much.

Satan whispers in your ear that close relationships are too painful. You buy the lie and say, "I won't ever get close to anyone else again."

Then the Holy Spirit whispers in your ear, "It is worth it. And while you may not feel it now, you will make the decision to rise up. And when you do, I'll be there to lift you."

Satan tells you it's too painful to get close to people. He does that to isolate you. Because when you are isolated, alone, empty, and depressed, you want to give up. But when you're surrounded by people who love you, they encourage you and refuse to let you give up.

So, is this deep connection of relationship worth the potential pain?

You bet it is!

There's no greater gift you can give yourself (and others) than the gift of love, and the gift of love includes the commitment to forgive.

Are you ready to make that commitment today? It's one of the best decisions you will ever make because it has a ripple effect.

The decision to choose forgiveness.

The decision to empower yourself.

The decision to fight the real enemy and not your loved ones.

The decision to choose your freedom and unlock the chains that have held you bound.

Just like those nurses held me as I took my first painful steps with bandaged, blistered, and painful feet, the Holy Spirit holds us as we take the first steps into forgiveness. In order to heal, we must make the decision and then commit to take the steps regardless of how we feel. Forgiveness is not a gift to someone else, it's the gift you give yourself.

APPLICATION

Are you ready to take the steps toward forgiveness?

How to Forgive:

1. Identify the pain and where it's rooted from. Get as specific as you need to.

2. Make the decision to forgive.

3. Cancel the debt. It is a debt that the offender can never pay back. When you cancel the debt you can move on.

You're likely going to have to repeat step three over and over and over again, reminding yourself that the debt was canceled.

When we don't forgive, we remain attached to the hurt and pain, and continue to carry the heaviness of the situation. But when we choose to forgive, we cut the weight from us. Are you choosing to remain connected to the pain or will you choose to break free?

We may not feel the release of the weight right away, but eventually we will.

If you would like to go a step further, write the offense down on a sheet of paper. Pray for the person who hurt you and say out loud that you've forgiven them and ask God to help you continue to live a life of forgiveness. Then rip that paper up into many small pieces and throw it in the trash as a symbol of the commitment to release the offense.

Let's make it personal...

What's that thing you've been hanging on to because you had the "right" to be angry and bitter?

Is hanging onto the unforgiveness helping you or hurting you?

What is it that keeps you hanging on and refusing to give yourself the gift of forgiveness?

Are you ready to release the pain and cut the ties that have kept you bound?

Have you gotten honest with God and really let him in on how you're feeling? The pain, the anger, the frustration, etc. Have an open conversation with God. He's a big God, he can handle what you're feeling and he knows anyway, so you might as well share it all with him so you can begin to heal. 1 John 1:9 attest to that fact that if we confess our sins, he is faithful and just and will forgive us our sins and *purify* us from all unrighteousness.

Chapter 15

The Scent Of A Woman

If You Hang Around Poo Long Enough...

My younger two (now teenage) sons were getting ready to leave to go to their first soccer game of the season. They wanted to eat before they left, and they wanted to be somewhat healthy, so they had subs. With lots and lots of onions.

I was just arriving home from a business meeting when they were hopping in the car to leave. I always make them hug me before they go anywhere (yup, I'm that freak mom!). So when I squeezed my youngest son and smelled something awful I said, "Dude you need to reapply deodorant before you leave, you can't be going out smelling like that." He said, "No mom it's the shirt!"

As I walked into the house, my other son was heading out the door and we crossed paths. I grabbed him to hug him and I got a whiff of the same bad smell. I asked him, "Bro what the heck smells so bad?" He said,

145

"Oh mom, that's just our sandwiches!" Sure enough, I walked into the kitchen and the onions hit my nose. It was like those old cartoons where the skunk's smell created a cloud that would hit with no warning. The onions from the sandwiches smelled like body odor.

The smell had consumed my kitchen, so I pitched all the wrappers and trash to try to clear the air a little bit. It took awhile, but eventually the smell disappeared.

That day of the infamous onion scented subs reminds me of something my mom used to say to my siblings and me, "If you hang around poo long enough you'll begin to smell like it." She was always checking up on who we were surrounding ourselves with. She wanted to make sure we hung around the nice, well behaved, wise decision making friends. She knew who we hung out with mattered.

But it wasn't just about getting into trouble. It was about attitude. When you hang out with people who have stinky attitudes, quick tempers, and are difficult to please, those negative traits rub off on you, just like onions in a stinky sub.

Scripture warns us to watch who we hang out with...

Proverbs 13:20 "Walk with the wise and become wise; associate with fools and get in trouble."

1 Corinthians 15:33 "Do not be misled: 'Bad company corrupts good character'."

And while my mom used to refer to bad company as smelly poo, she knew what she was talking about.

Misery loves company. Negative attitudes and minds all stick together— the naysayers, the doomsdayers, the worst case scenario people— they all hang out together. When you go into a room full of negative people, even if you're a positive optimistic person, it drains you.

It's kinda like my kids going into the restaurant to order their sandwiches before the game. Before they had even eaten the sandwiches, they picked up the onion aroma, thanks to being in the restaurant where the scent was super heavy. When they walked out, they still smelled like that oniony restaurant. And then, when they ate those sandwiches...it took it to a whole new level. That smell even came to our home and stunk up our kitchen. There was no outrunning that stank!

That onion stink is also like the stink of negativity that comes from complainers. You probably know one or two of these individuals. They are the kind of people that complain about everything. Here's the thing about complaining though, you can complain as much as you want about something, and it doesn't change a thing. The smell is still there. We have to wash down our attitudes, our thoughts, and our talk in order to change that yucky scent that somehow attached itself to us. And that's what complaining does. It grabs on to you like a yucky skunk smell and it takes a lot of work to get completely rid of it. It's not impossible to do though, it just takes a lot of discipline. Wanna know how? Apply the steps learned in The Labelmaker (see chapter two). That's a great way to implement the attitude change.

Have you ever walked by someone wearing a pleasant smelling perfume? You breathe it in and wonder, "Oh what is that mahhhh-velous scent?" You want to continue to smell it because there's something attractive about it. A scent isn't just about the nose. A scent is also intuition. It's love and romance. It's attitude. Whatever the aroma in a room, if you stay there long enough, you will begin to wear that scent.

The best is when you greet someone wearing an amazing scent and they hug you really tight...By the way, I'm typically not a lingering hugger. I'll give a quick squeeze and go. But when you're hugging someone wearing an amazing perfume, you don't want to let go because you know that when you hug them, their perfume will linger on you. Then you'll carry that scent with you and soon people are noticing how great you smell as a result!

Likewise, you become the one that shares the great aroma with everyone you hug. It goes from one person to the next—a pleasing aroma that is passed around. In many ways, it's similar to what happens when a group of women who are empowering one another gather together. You know what kind of women I'm talking about - those who lift each other up and encourage each other. Who bring out the best in one another.

A few years ago I was a part of a group of women like that. It was a year long mentoring group with business women from all over the US and Canada. We got together for a weekend and it was an amazing display of encouragement and passing the aroma of greatness around. When one woman expressed doubt in herself, the others all would say, "No girl, you got this." Then another woman would dream out loud and all the other ladies in the room would oooh and ahhh and say, "YES, you can do that!" We were all pushing one another to dream bigger and go harder. Every woman in the room was carrying around a fresh, "you got this!" aroma. The scents of empowerment and encouragement now have the possibility to continue to touch endless lives as the aroma is left behind wherever these ladies go. That's a scent that needs to linger and be shared.

My mother-in-law used to wear a particular perfume, and you didn't have to be anywhere near her to smell it. She left the scent behind, so no matter where she was, you knew where she'd been because she left the lovely scent of her perfume behind. In that same way, we can leave behind the scent of empowerment, encouragement, love, and hope to others. Doesn't that aroma smell wonderful?

APPLICATION

Scripture makes it very clear (and in some cases warns us) that who we surround ourselves with does matter. Surround yourself with those who will loving challenge you, who will empower you and help build better character, motivating you to leave a refreshing scent everywhere you go.

Proverbs 27:17 "As iron sharpens iron, so a friend sharpens a friend."

Proverbs 22:24-25 "Do not be a friend of one who has a bad temper, and never keep company with a hothead, or you will learn his ways and set a trap for yourself."

Proverbs 16:29 "A violent person entices their neighbor and leads them down a path that is not good."

Proverbs 12:26 "The righteous choose their friends carefully, but the way of the wicked leads them astray."

Now let's make it personal…

Are you making your friends better?

Are your friends making you better?

When you leave a conversation, after spending time with someone, are you leaving behind a scent that they want to hold on to? Or are you leaving behind a scent so nasty they feel like they need to go launder their clothes and take a shower?

Our words, our attitudes, our actions... all of them leave a scent. You have the ability to make the world smell better, to feel better and to bring joy. When you walk away do you make people feel better?

Have you improved their lives?

When you leave, how are they feeling?

When it comes to those in your closest circle...When they leave you, do you feel like there is a stench in the air? Or does it smell better because they were there? Do YOU smell better because you were hugging all over them?

It's true. Whatever you hang out with you begin to smell like. It's time to get real...what's your scent?

Chapter 16

Dropping The F-Bomb

Love Without Limits

Girl puh-lease! Get your mind outta the gutter. I ain't going there! Just hang with me and keep reading, you'll pick up what I'm throwing down in a few more paragraphs.

It happened over twenty years ago. My then boyfriend (now husband) and I had only been dating for a few weeks. It was August and it was hot. We had driven to Indiana to visit my future brother-in-law and his family for the day. You know those early stages of dating where you're super giddy? Everything you both do is cute to each other. He could've had a speck of black pepper in his teeth and I'd have found it adorable.

To me, this guy was different. He was ten years older than me, he had two boys that were so adorable, and I really just fell in love with all three of them. I didn't want to fall too hard, too fast, although it was a little too late. I didn't want to mess this up. I was also determined to be 100% myself, but at the same time not too much myself because I knew I could be a bit much. Like that one time on a blind date when I put in fake jacked up teeth that looked real and I left them in for a few minutes. I thought it was a hilarious ice breaker, but I never heard from that guy again. Clearly he wasn't meant for me. I knew I could be a lot, and typically I didn't care.

I was usually that girl that passed gas in front of the guy first. It didn't matter to me. Take me or leave me, I pass gas. If a dude couldn't handle it, it was his problem not mine. But not with this guy. I was kinda digging him and I wanted to leave a good impression.

So there we were, sitting in his black Jeep Grand Cherokee with the windows down, in a parking lot at his brother's apartment building, overlooking a pond, watching ducks. Our feet were dangling out the windows as we were shooting the breeze, laughing, giggling, and just being giddy.

Then he ripped one. I laughed so hard my stomach was cramping.

Why is it that farting is always funny? Like no matter what, you can fart and it's funny. Except at the dinner table. Then it's not funny. But any other time, it's funny.

154

Sitting in church and it's quiet...a little one peeps out— HILARIOUS. And, since you're not supposed to laugh, it becomes that much funnier.

Or, when you were in class at school and someone ripped one, a riot of laughter always erupted.

It never fails. Farts are always funny.

So he had let one loose, and we were both rolling and my stomach was hurting from laughing so hard. This was in my twenties and BC (before children) so I didn't have any bladder issues to contend with. The worst thing that happened when I laughed back then was that my abs hurt and I built up more muscles (cry me a river right?) anyway...

Out of nowhere he looked at me and said, "Why don't you fart in front of me?"

What the heck? He was asking me to drop the f-bomb in front of him right here, right now? Like, isn't that awkward? I thought it would happen by accident. You know, it'd just oopsy-dentally slip out at some point, but this guy was actually asking me to fart in front of him.

I said, "Dude, you have no idea. Like, once we go there, there's no going back. And you will likely wish there was going back."

"Noooooooo!" He exclaimed. "It'll be cool, just fart in front of me, I just wanna hear you rip one."

What he didn't realize was that I came from a family of seven kids and that belching and farting were like

Olympic sports, and I was the gold medalist of 1981 and 1994 (and definitely made the podium every year because I was that good) so I was fresh off of Olympic wins. OK. If this is what he was asking for, why should I deny him of my natural giftings?

I did my best to talk him out of it and I did tell him that once this door was opened, it would not be closed. That once I farted in front of him, I would never withhold my gas ever again. Unless of course it was at dinner, and even then it wasn't guaranteed. The only guarantee was if we were in public, or with someone else, then I'd hold back. Other than that, it was game on.

I've never seen someone so excited to hear the release of gas before. His anticipation was like a little child about to experience their first bite of candy. And I must say, I don't believe it disappointed. I was proud of my gold medal performance and continued on. However, it ended up like a child getting too much candy and the sugar upset his stomach. Only it wasn't sugar. It was gas.

I had told him. I had warned him. But there was no going back.

Here we are twenty plus years later. I'm still just as gassy as ever. I even like to play a game of turtle every now and again. At night when we're in bed, I will let one slip and it's not until he gets a whiff of it does he realize what happened. Every once in a while my little ornery giggle will give it away, but most of the time he doesn't catch on until he gets the whiff of my gifting.

He asked for it. I warned him. I was me. I'm still me. He wanted to see what I think is the grossest part of me...And when he saw it, he still loved me. Every bit of me.

You know, I believe that's how God is with us. He sees the nastiest, most embarrassing (even shameful) parts of us and He still loves us regardless. When everyone else is grossed out or embarrassed, He still loves us.

The thing is, my then boyfriend, now hubby, asked me to be me. The real, true 100% authentic me...and I wanted to be the real me. I can't fake who I am everyday of the week, twenty-four hours a day. It may not be gas. Some days it's me being grumpy. Some days it's me needing to cry. Some moments it's me being scared. I have to be honest in who I am. And if I can't be me with those who are closest to me, then who can I be real with?

Do you find yourself surrounded with people who you feel like you have to impress or live up to a certain standard around them? If so, you will (if you're not already) end up trying to live up to the perceived expectations that others have for you instead of living out your true, authentic self. The only way you can live a life of joy is to be true to who God created you to be.

Here's another example—as much as I love people, I need my alone time. My family knows that, so they don't expect me to be around people all the time. They also don't expect me to be comedian Holly all the time either. They allow me to feel all the feels and that means sometimes being sad, grumpy, irritated, and other times happy. They let me be human and they love me beyond my imperfections.

The last thing you need to do is worry about performing for others and trying to live to impress everyone else, or be something or someone that someone else wants you to be. All you need to do is be who God called you to be. Yes, you should be constantly working to better yourself— not for the approval of others, but to live a life in the fullness of God's love and to achieve your highest calling!

Case in point — I'm not writing this book to impress anyone or to get a certain group of people to like me. I'm writing this book for you, to offer insight and share wisdom, and to give you permission to feel different emotions. If, after you find out that I fart and laugh about it, (and may even brag about it) you are grossed out and never want to hear me speak or read another thing I write, then that's OK. You can find someone that aligns better with your personality. I am who I am. I am going to continue to walk in laughter and love because that's what God has called me to do and He created me with this ornery streak!

You should not change who you are for anyone. Again, let me clarify, yes you want to better yourself and work on your weaknesses, but you should not change your core values at the leading of anyone other than God himself. Only change as the Holy Spirit guides and directs you. It's a liberating feeling to know that you don't have to live to impress others. I hope you'll join me in living to impress God and God alone.

I also hope that you will embrace yourself 100%. The good, the bad, the ugly, the beautiful, and the glorious. That you would love those in your circle the same way you want to be loved— beyond imperfections and see God's wonderful creation in each other. We weren't created for everybody. However, you were created for those who are closest to you. Embrace yourself and your loved ones. They are your people and you are theirs. You are God's gift to each other.

APPLICATION

Recognize that God loves you so much that He sent his only Son for you. Find scriptures to study that support His love for you. If you are new to this or don't have a Bible, just Google "verses about God's love for me" and write down the ones that you connect with. #Ijustgaveyouhomework

I will start you off with this one verse:

"Such love has no fear, because perfect love expels all fear. If we are afraid, it is for fear of punishment, and this shows that we have not fully experienced his perfect love." 1 John 4:18 (NLT)

The verse says fear of punishment. But let's re-read the verse and put in that word that suits your fear. Are you facing fear of rejection, insecurity, unforgiveness, resentment, fill in the blank. But once we experience His perfect love and learn to remain in it, all fear is gone. It's possible!

You are worthy of this love. Not only that, you are worthy of the love of those in your life. We were created to live life together. Surround yourself with people who believe in you, who will lovingly correct you and who truly care for you. Fill your circle with those who love unconditionally and share Christ's unconditional love with them.

Now let's make it personal...

Are there areas in your life that you find yourself compromising who you are for the sake of someone else's approval? In what areas and how are you compromising?

How have those compromises shown up in your life?

It's easy to fall into the trap- it's a slow fade. Can you see where it first began and how it got you to where you are now? How did it happen?

What are you gaining from this person's approval/praise?

What will you gain from living for God instead of people?

Ok now that you did your homework, what are the differences between God's love for you and the love you are seeking from others?

Chapter 17

Crazy Mama Bear In A Minivan

Ethical and Egotistical Anger

I was in my van with my youngest two boys, one was about three and the other was almost one. We were driving through the parking lot at the mall in my super cool gray Nissan Quest minivan. Hey, I gotta try to make the minivan game sound strong, can I get a witness? So, there I was, driving slow through the mall, when a little sedan filled with teenagers came whipping around me and almost hit my van full of priceless cargo. Needless to say, I was LIVID!

My blood was pumping, my eyes were wide open, and this mama had her foot on the pedal as I followed these young punks, ahem, I mean young kids, who clearly needed a lesson. I followed them as they pulled into their parking spot, and I stopped my van right behind them. They couldn't escape me. I was like a mama bear going after a hunter that missed a shot aimed for her young. Hey, I don't claim to have reacted logically here, clearly this was the emotional response of an overprotective mama. #Dontmesswithmykids (BOOM-- I'm so hard core that I'm still using hashtags where they don't belong!)

I left my van running with my boys in it (just because I was protective didn't mean I was always smart), and I hopped out of that van and marched over to the driver's window with the full intent of giving them a piece of my mind.

I started knocking on the window like a madwoman. A teenager, with a look of sheer horror on his face rolled down the window.

"Did you NOT see me?" I was YELLING at this poor kid.

"You almost hit my van and I have my boys in it!"

I was livid and I was letting them know. I was also not afraid of laying it on thick to let them know the impact their stupid decision could have had on my life.

"I just buried my daughter five years ago, you think I want to bury my boys now too? Thanks to you I could have!"

The look of sheer horror turned into a look of panic.

"You're lucky you didn't hit me."

At this point, I realized that my emotions were waaaaaaaay out of control and these were just normal teenagers out having fun. They weren't a bunch of punks up to no good. They were just at the mall. And truth be told, they were likely better drivers at that age than I was.

So I had to reign it in really quickly. I took a deep breath and said a silent prayer that Jesus would shut my mouth and open my heart.

"Ma'am I'm really sorry, I didn't mean to..." He started to apologize.

"Listen, I realize you're teenagers." I started to choke up a bit and began to feel overwhelmed with regret in my mishandling of the situation.

My tone changed from tense, psycho-mom anger, to soft correction.

"I didn't mean to go off on you like that. Seriously, I get it. You're out having fun. But be aware of your surroundings. Pay attention to who is around. You're young, you think you are immortal and that nothing can happen to you. Please, just remember you're driving a machine that while is a ton of fun, it can also be very dangerous. All I ask is that you be responsible and slow it down a bit. OK?"

Still with a look of panic and fear on his face, the young man looked up at me, nodded his head up and down, and gave me a simple "Yes, Ma'am."

With my psychotic episode behind me, and having taught those kids a lesson (or two), I calmly walked back to my van and drove away shaking. And then I bawled the whole ride home.

So, what does this story have to do with joy? Well, in an earlier chapter, we went through how to label any situation to make it work for you. If you're like most people (or maybe it's just me) there are still things that honk you off. I mean, like really make you mad. Such as a carload of teenagers driving through a parking lot like it's a raceway.

Now I want to ask you a personal and a bit of a deep question. Let's pretend we're sitting on your couch, all nice and comfy, coffee (or tea) in hand, me in yoga pants and an oversized bright colored tee, and you in your most fave comfy attire.

Now listen girlfriend, it's only you, me, and God listening in, and if you want to start overflowing with joy, then we gotta get down and dirty for just a moment. I promise, I'll do my best to keep it as painless as possible. But in order to get the splinter out where it's sore and festering under the skin, I gotta grab the tweezers and dig for a moment.

What is the one thing you're most angry about right now? How long have you been dealing with it?

You know what I'm talking about. It's that thing that you've been angry about for a while. You keep trying to shake it off, but you haven't been able to. Maybe it's that person who refuses to change and you're all frustrated...which leads to more anger. Or, maybe it's a situation that doesn't seem to get resolved, no matter what you do or what steps you take...You can't solve it by yourself and that makes you angrier. I want to help you out, so I'm about to get all up in your personal biz and ask you...

Do you consider yourself more of an ethical person—looking at what's right for the general population (your family, your team, your co-workers)?

Or...

Do you think you're generally an egotistical person— looking out for your personal best interests?

Or do you fall somewhere in between?

As human beings we want to convince ourselves that we are considerate of others and that we aren't self-serving, but we also need to be honest with ourselves and assess where we're really at.

Let's go back to your situation. What has you stirring in your spirit? What is that thing that you're so angry about? Now, before we dive into this anger I want to first share with you the fact that anger in and of itself isn't a bad thing.

Anger is a God given emotion to benefit us. It tells us that something is wrong somewhere and needs to be corrected.

However, when I make my anger self serving, then I'm not using it in the way God intended. God gave us the emotion of anger so that we could fix the injustices of this world (not just our individual worlds).

Let's get real girlfriend, sometimes my anger isn't about the social injustices of this world but *my* world! And I get mad. Like really mad. Like when I want my husband to go to a specific restaurant after I've told him that "I don't care" where we go. Every place he suggests, I shoot down. Finally, I convince him to make a stinking decision. He does what I tell him to. He makes a decision. He just happens to pick a place he wants and I can't stand.

Let me tell you, that does not happen very often. My husband is easy going and somehow over the years I've turned into a bit of a food snob (at least that's what I've heard). I mean, some restaurants just make me sick. Not actually sick, like vomiting or anything like that, but sick in the sense of feeling yucky and bloated after I eat there. The older I've gotten, the more sensitive my stomach has become, and so I have acquired more expensive taste in restaurants.

Meanwhile, my hubby can eat junk. I'm talking gas station chili dogs for breakfast with processed cheese on top. And he washes it down with a soda. Of course he doesn't gain a pound. His weight has fluctuated the same ten pounds our entire marriage, while I've literally lost and gained the sum of his entire weight over the course of our marriage.

So anyway, back to the restaurant. On the very rare occasion that he picks a restaurant he really wants, I can feel this irritability rising up in me. I mean, he knows how this place makes me sick, right?

So I get angry. Sometimes I do the old silent treatment and say everything's "Fine." and give him one word sentences. While other times, I have fought through the anger to suck it up. But let's be honest, either way, when I don't get what I want, if I don't keep my flesh in check, I can get angry.

This is what I refer to as Egotistical Anger.

Egotistical Anger is all about me not getting my way, what I want, or what I thought I deserved. It's self-centered and it's the flesh acting out.

Maybe for you it's not a restaurant. Maybe it's a lack of control. Maybe it's not getting a particular expectation met. Maybe it's someone who you were counting on to do you a favor and leverage their clout to surprise you with that item you've been dying to have...And they didn't get it for you. You feel angry, and entitled to your anger. That's egotistical anger that you're experiencing.

Then on the flipside, there's the side of me that gets angry when I see someone picking on one of my sons. Maybe they look at them the wrong way, they say the wrong thing, or they target them not because they have done something wrong, but just because kids can be

169

mean sometimes. And when that happens, watch out! Mama Bear is on the loose.

Maybe for you it's not a mama bear thing. Maybe it's that you were left out of a party invite with a bunch of friends.

Or maybe it's impoverished kids, animal cruelty, or parents who neglect their kids that gets your blood boiling.

That is called Ethical Anger.

Ethical Anger is what is stirred up in us to correct the injustices in the world.

Anger tells us there is something wrong that needs to be corrected. If that wrong is selfish and coming from an inward motivation, that is Egotistical Anger and needs to be put in check.

Ethical anger is about correcting an injustice (it can be for yourself) but it's not motivated by selfish desires. Instead it is fueled by holy righteous anger — a desire to fix the injustice.

If you want to be full of joy, it doesn't mean you'll lack anger. Joyful people can get angry, however their anger isn't egotistical, instead it's ethical. And when they stand up for the underdog, that creates a stronger sense of purpose... which then builds confidence, which ultimately creates even more of a sense of joy!

Let's go back to your situation. That thing you're so upset about and having a difficult time getting to the other side of...Is it healthy, ethical anger? Or could it possibly be damaging, egotistical anger?

I want you to get real with yourself. As you rehash the situation, are you mad because there is something unjust going on? Or are you angry because you're not getting what you wanted (or thought you deserved)?

When you get honest with yourself, you can really begin to work through it.

When my husband picks a restaurant I can't stand and I get upset, I've learned to just tell myself it's not that big of a deal and it will be ok. It's not always easy keeping my flesh in check, but I have to. Otherwise I can ruin what was supposed to be a great night out.

The enemy wants to rob of us of our joy. One of the best ways he does it is by getting us all caught up in our self-centered flesh. If we're selfish enough, we have the ability to also make an impact on those around us and rob them of their joy. So this anger thing...yeah, it's a biggie.

APPLICATION

The next time you feel anger rising up don't forget that we are encouraged in James 1:19 to "be quick to listen, slow to speak, and slow to become angry." (Let me tell ya, that's one you are gonna want to tuck away. There are days you are going to *need* it!) Sometimes that will help check our anger.

171

Then ask yourself, is this egotistical anger or ethical anger that's stirring up? If it's egotistical anger, you need to check yourself before you wreck yourself. If it's ethical anger, then move forward according to the leading of the Holy Spirit. Most of the time a resolution isn't about you changing someone or their behavior, but it's about you changing your direction or positioning.

Reflect on the situation that you're currently angry about. What is it that angers you? Is it an injustice? Is it that you didn't get what you wanted?

Perhaps it may be a little of both.

Take some time to journal your thoughts to get to the bottom of the true motivation behind your anger. Once revealed, you can determine whether to let it go, or what measures need to be taken to resolve the issue.

Let's make it personal...

Is egotistical anger something you struggle with?

What are some examples of times you've felt egotistical anger?

What are some experiences you've had when you've felt ethical anger?

Is there a different feeling with these two types of anger?

What type of results did you get with egotistical anger? How did they make you feel? How did they make your loved ones feel?

What type of results did you get with ethical anger? How did they make you feel? How did they make your loved ones feel?

Chapter 18

Tone Deaf

Setting the Tone

Back when I was pastoring, one of the things I would get to do every once in a while was kids' check-in for children's church and the nursery.

One morning I was doing check-in at kids' church, which was right next to the nursery, and I could hear a little baby crying. We had a fabulous team of nursery volunteers so I knew this little one was in good hands. As this baby was crying, a mom and her two little ones came up to check in. They too could hear the cry of the baby from the nursery (which happened to be where the little sister was about to go). The little sister looked at her big sister with a scared expression on her face. And that's when it happened.

The six-year-old, who was the older, experienced, and wiser sister said to her almost three-year-old baby sister, "Do you hear that? You can go in and cheer that baby up!"

This big sister heard the cry of the baby and instead of being alarmed and saying, "you shouldn't go in there, that sounds scary," she encouraged baby sis to go on in and make a difference.

TALK ABOUT PERSPECTIVE! (Sorry for yelling, I just got a little excited!)

We have been called to be a light, to be a city on a hill... to spread His love. My sweet sister, is that what you're doing? Or have you become a complainer?

The complainer complains about everything. It could be seventy-two degrees and sunny and they are complaining because it's too bright. It could be seventy-two degrees and cloudy and that same Negative Nelly is nagging because it's too dark out. There's nothing that's ever good enough in the life of a complainer.

Then there's the backhanded optimist. This person talks about how wonderful life is, but still finds a way to throw a complaint in the mix. "Oh my, I'm so blessed, God's been so good to me, He's so good to me that I've got six kids that are just wonderful, they wear me down and wear me out but I'm wonderful!" Sometimes y'all we're just tired. And it's OK to say I'm exhausted. I'm not talking about that. I'm talking about the constant complainer. You know this person...nothing but complaints are coming out of their mouth, even when they try to make them sound like they're blessings.

Raise your hand if you've ever been guilty of being that backhanded optimist? (I quietly raise my hand; Lord knows I've been there before).

Thinking back to that day at kids' church, that six-year-old little girl preached a sermon and she didn't even know it!

Our world (the nursery) is full of chaos, pain, and confusion, or as the Bible says, "tribulation". HOWEVER, these words came from Jesus Himself.

"I have said these things to you, that in me you may have peace. In the world you will have tribulation. But take heart; I have overcome the world." John 16:33 (ESV).

Merriam Webster gives us this simple definition of overcome:

: to defeat (someone or something)

: to successfully deal with or gain control of (something difficult)

: to affect (someone) very strongly or severely

If you are stuck in Negative Nelly Mode, I want you to write this down, "In the world you will have tribulation. **BUT** take heart; I have overcome the world." John 16:33

So Jesus has already overcome the world. Even if it doesn't feel like it right now, that makes YOU are an overcomer too.

Hold your head high today dear sister... YOU ARE A WINNER! So when tough times come and you are feeling defeated, remember God sees the other side.

Here's how you can make it happen in your day-to-day lives. As a woman, you set the emotional tone in your home. No one can impact a home quite like mama. Ever heard that phrase "Happy wife, happy life" or "Happy mom, life is calm"? Ok I just made the second one up... but it's true and it rhymes! I may end up spitting out a few rhymes in the lines of this chapter too!

Sister, YOU set the emotional tone in your home.

I remember something important that one of my friends told me a long time ago, before my youngest two kids had started attending school. She told me the importance of starting your day off right, not just for me, but for the sake of my family.

Man was this so true.

I would notice on the days that we were running behind or I was stressed, I was more irritated, less patient, and my kids were the ones that paid for it. Yes, unfortunately I was a yeller. It's not something I'm proud of, and I really try to keep it in check now.

So moms, I wanna speak specifically to you right here, right now. One of the things I wanted to share in this book is how to set the tone for your day and for your family.

Can I tell you that there are certain practices that help you no matter what? These ten ideas below may seem super simple but if you implement them into your daily life you will see a difference. I betcha might even be able to help your friends make simple changes that can transform the tone of their lives as well. So whether it's in your home, your office, your group of friends...

wherever it is that God gave you influence over others, you can help guide them in finding simple changes that will help set them up for the win!

1. Give yourself plenty of time in the morning. You need time to not only get ready, but more importantly, have some quiet time before everyone else gets up.

2. During that quiet time, the most important thing you could be doing is spending time with God. Read His word, pray, and listen to worship music. Spending time with Him is the first step to setting the right tone for the rest of the day. When you're in tune with Him, you're more in the spirit than you are the flesh and you're better equipped to handle whatever is thrown at you that day. And let's face it, you're getting some pretty crazy things thrown at you.

3. Give your family ample time in the morning to get ready. I used to let my youngest sleep in as late as possible because he needed the most amount of sleep. However, he is super laid back and moves at a slower steady pace, so I couldn't ever get him to move fast enough. It was setting us up for failure every morning. I needed to realize that he moves slow and that unless there is a fire or

some sort of major emergency, he wasn't going to speed up. So, I started getting him up earlier and it saved us both a huge headache.

4. When things get heated, have a code word that means we need to take a few minutes to calm down. I encourage everyone to choose a word that is totally unrelated to stress, like the word Pineapple. If one of you hollars out "PINEAPPLE!!!" in the middle of a conversation, it can actually lighten the mood. And it also lets you know that you both need to take a few minutes to calm down and then return to the topic at hand when the emotions have settled a bit.

5. Don't yell at your kids or your spouse before they go off to school or work. Save the difficult conversations for when you have time to discuss everything in love, and get that fifteen minute break to cool down if you need it.

6. This next one is actually one of my all-time fave guidelines that my husband came up with. No heavy conversations after 8:00 p.m. It used to be 10:00 p.m. but we're getting older and more tired so we had to make it earlier. Pick a time for you and your spouse and agree that there will be no heavy conversations after that time and stick to

it. We know in our household that by 8:00 p.m. most of us are exhausted. An exhausted state is not the time when you want to be having heavy conversations and making big decisions. So pick a time for those discussions and make sure they are uninterrupted. There have been times where fights could have been picked, but because of this rule, the arguments were avoided. When you're tired you tend to be more emotional, so picking a time that you agree upon, will set you up for a better conversation because it's taking place when you're well rested and not so emotional. This also means coming up with solutions can be a lot easier.

7. Don't give anyone power over your mood. No one can ruin your day unless you let them. Yes, you can have a bad moment, but a bad moment left unchecked will turn into a bad morning. A bad morning turns into a bad day. A bad day turns into a bad week. And so on. However, the opposite holds true as well. You can have a bad moment and choose to let it go. Then, you can still have a good morning, which turns into a good day. Which then becomes a good week, and then a good month, and then before ya know it, you've had a great year! You've got the power, make sure you use it for good!

8. Make sure you spend a minimum of fifteen minutes a day with uninterrupted, tech free conversation with your loved ones. Put all phones in a basket, TV off, no tablets. Nothing but face to face communication. I say a minimum of fifteen minutes because that's a great place to start. Work your way up to as high as you want to go. If nothing else, keep the dinner table tech free. In our house, we always ask for high points and low points at dinner. It gives us a chance to hear how everyone's day has gone. This is a great conversation starter. Not to mention, it keeps you in the loop as to what is going on in each other's lives.

9. Never go to bed angry or holding onto unforgiveness. And always end each day with a quick kiss and an, "I love you" to your loved ones. We truly don't know when it could be the last one and you'll never regret showing your family love.

10. Smile. Keep smiling. Randomly smile at strangers, and as weird as it may sound, smile at those who are closest to you. Too often we are more kind to strangers than we are our own families. Show those closest to you that kindness matters. Choose kindness, grace, and a smile. Everyone can always use a little more kindness and grace.

Now, you can't be everything to everyone. Don't set yourself up with that kind of pressure. Not every child in the nursery is gonna love it when you come to play. And that's ok, there's other people for them.

In the last fifteen years I've been many things to many people. And I've tried so hard to be what "they" needed. I was stretched so thin that I wasn't good to anyone. I'd been so many things to so many different people that I'd lost being who I was called to be.

As you begin to make changes in your life that allow you to hear a baby's cry and point out opportunity for a win, there are going to be people who are offended by that fire in your soul. There were times where I felt like I needed to dim my passion in order to make the person I was standing next to feel comfortable with their shine. It wasn't just one person who somehow made me feel like this, it was something I'd picked up along the way. I unconsciously learned to dim my light to help others shine brighter. I dimmed my light so much and so often that my fire was almost burnt out. I believed the lie that I needed to make myself appear to be dumber, quieter, more ignorant, less confident... all to make others feel better about themselves.

God doesn't want us to get caught up worrying about the brightness of everyone's lights. He wants us to shine! You were designed with your own special color and light. Every single woman has her own appealing glow. God created you with gifts and talents that are unique to you and your style. Use them. Don't dim your light to avoid threatening or outshining someone else. We're not here to outshine anyone, we're here to bring light to the world. So shine brightly and confidently my dear sister, we need your light! Together we can illuminate the world!

People are going to think what they want to think no matter what you do. Not only are we battling our own negativity, we quickly accept the negativity of others-- which leads to defeat, not victory. And that's why I had you jot down that verse. Revisit it till it's carved in that pretty, little head of yours.

Picture this. You're hanging out by the pool with some friends. You don't have your kids with you, so you're relaxing with your favorite book in one hand and a refreshing beverage in the other. You look up and you see a toddler struggling in the pool. Suddenly your adrenaline is pumping, and it's as if you're the only one who notices what is going on in the middle of the quiet waters. You become fully aware that the toddler needs to be rescued. Everyone else around you is just staring - watching as you jump in after this little one—a child you don't even know, yet you're diving in as if it's your own. As you get out of the pool, you make sure the child is OK. The parents are notified and everyone is good. The child is fine. The parents are a bit frazzled. They weren't being irresponsible, the child just got away from them and they didn't realize it. It could happen to anyone.

You sit back down only to realize, you're a friggin hero! You just saved a child's life! You're like, "YES!" You feel empowered and like a rock star.

Then a complete stranger, not knowing you, the situation, or the child comes up to you and says, "You know, you really should watch your kids. I can't believe you just did that, letting your kid just go into the water alone like that. Who do you think you are? What the heck are you doing letting that child wander around here all by himself?"

They are assuming the child is your responsibility, and that it's your fault. Instances like this is where we learn to dim our lights. But listen up... everyone else is seeing the fact that you just saved a child's life. And ONE person is upset because they think you let the child wander into the pool.

Can I tell you that's how life is? Those who are in your circle, your life, they are totally supporting you and cheering you on for being the hero that you are. Don't listen to the one Negative Nelly in the crowd! There will always be at least one person that chooses to see only the negativity. That's not your person. That negative comment can hold you down like a brick holds down a helium balloon. You need to cut them loose. Let them go and fly on sister!

APPLICATION

Remember that little girl I talked about in the beginning of this chapter? Do you want to be like her and go out and cheer somebody on? Cheer somebody up? All that matters is that you spread cheer! You are light and God wants you to shine. Everyone might not like your light or it's brightness, but remember you are here to win! So drown out all those other voices, maybe even your own, and hear the Spirit say, "Take heart, I have overcome!" Follow His lead and you too will overcome all the heartache and troubles and rest in His everlasting joy, which in turn will give the Source of your light, the glory He deserves.

Now let's make it personal...

What's your "go to" tone?

How can you set a better tone in your home?

Take a moment and ask God to give you tangible steps that can be implemented in your home. (They may be some I listed or He may give you new ones unique to your home.)

You are not responsible for everyone else, but sister, the light God has given you over your loved ones can help guide them and teach them. How can you use this light wisely?

If someone or something has happened to you that has taught you to dim your light. Write it down as a sign of letting go. (God may bring this to your mind as you read others chapters of the book, especially when dealing with forgiveness.)

Chapter 19

Dancing Like Carlton

What If, What Is & Even If

My husband and I were attending the wedding of one of his college buddy's kids. It was a hot summer day, the wedding was outside, and I was the fluffiest (a gentle word for the biggest) I'd been since giving birth to my youngest who was, incidentally, fourteen years old. To make matters worse, I was struggling with a serious bout of poison ivy. Yeah, sounds like nothing until you find out that it's actually on the INSIDE of your body! Thanks to the steroids that gave me the appetite of my sixteen-year-old athletic son, combined with the sluggish metabolism of a mid-forties woman, and I was legit, the biggest I'd been in years.

Let's just say my confidence was not off the charts. However, I was not going to let my extra hard-earned, thirty-pound weight gain keep me from having the time of my life (cue song)!I bought a cute blush colored dress that fell to the floor, covering any imperfections, (and let's not forget the all-important Spanx to smooth out the rolls under my dress). Let me be real...I had enough rolls to open a bakery shop. Nevertheless, I fixed myself up, and felt as confident as possible, thanks to Spanx and a dress to compliment my curvaceousness.

As we waited for the wedding to begin while directly facing the powerful evening sun, I looked around and noticed a gorgeous millennial with a killer body. Until now, she had zero sweat, her body was perfect, her hair was on point, and her outfit showed off every perfection in her physique. I elbowed my husband, "Babe, freakin' look at her— she's gorgeous! How can someone be so perfect?" My husband awkwardly did not want to look at her (we have this respect thing going on where we don't check out other people). But I'm like, "Dude, seriously, I'm not trying to be weird or make you feel uncomfortable, but this woman is a masterpiece from God. Everyone notices the beauty in God's creation." As I was having this conversation with my husband I could feel the sweat dripping down my back. Now, how do I describe this without getting TMI? Basically, the sweat was dripping in cracks and crevices of my body that I didn't even know existed. I could feel it under my boobs. Hello boob sweat, that's hot (pun intended)! And then I felt it dripping down into the crack of my back...where it meets the cheeks, if ya know what I'm saying. I looked down at my stomach and saw a few darker spots from where sweat had seeped through my Spanx and into my dress.

I have to admit, I did get a bit of relief seeing the perfect twenty-something in front of me when her back displayed a light sparkle of perspiration from the heat. Here I was sweating bullets profusely, and she was merely glistening! While she looked beautiful with her shimmer, at least I felt somewhat normal, knowing it wasn't just my over-productive sweat glands.

We sat there through the wedding ceremony for what seemed like the longest twenty minutes of my life. Though the ceremony was beautiful, I was ready to get in the air conditioning. I reached a point where I'd become slap happy. It reminded me of being in church as a kid and my dad would tell me to be quiet, but then the giggles hit. Yeah, there I was, fighting back the urge to bust a gut rolling. My husband was giving me hilarious looks, and I was trying not to laugh at everything.

After what felt like forever, the ceremony finally ended and the wedding guests were dismissed row by row. As we went to leave, I looked around and saw that most people were perspiring. I went to straighten out my dress and it became painfully clear that I wasn't just perspiring, no, I'd had buckets dripping down my light colored dress, and there was a perfect line of sweat right where my butt crack was.

This is where the unconditional love of your spouse becomes ever so important.

I INSTANTLY grabbed my husband and firmly told him to walk behind me. He was clueless until he looked

191

down and saw the pinstripe of sweat directly down my lower back. He did what any wonderful, amazing, supportive husband would do, and he walked close behind to cover my embarrassing episode. Fortunately, we got a seat at the end table, where I sat down to rejoice that what could have been the most humiliating episode of my life was thwarted by my heroic husband! Crisis averted!

As the night went on we began to laugh at the situation... a lot! My husband has a twin, and they were both in attendance along with my sister-in-law. What you need to know is that my husband and his brother are beyond hysterical when they get together. It's literally non-stop laughing, which typically isn't a problem. On this night though, it was. You see, my adorable blush colored dress was made from a super thin cotton material. I wasn't wearing underwear but, I did have on a pantyliner, (sorry if that's too much for ya) and I've had four pregnancies, which equals absolutely zero bladder control. So every time we would laugh, which was literally every five minutes, I would pee a little! I knew what was going on, so before I needed a bucket for my leakage I was thinking I should head to the restroom, but it was already beyond too late. I had a wet spot on the back of my dress the size of a medium pizza. No joke!

Well, since, it was time for the toast, I figured I'd best go ahead and get control of my already out of control bladder issue. So I snuck to the bathroom, hoping to release any remaining fluids and try to clean up the mess from the previously released liquids during my fits of laughter.

Listen, at this point I knew it was so far gone. Even still, I knew I needed to sit down, air out my dress for a moment, and perhaps all would be well. I figured that if the dress got aired out a bit, then my Spanx would begin to dry up as well.

Just as I returned from the bathroom an INCREDIBLE song came on. My sis-in-law said, "Let's go girl! We gotta hit the floor!" My husband decided it was time for him to hit the restroom, conveniently timed to avoid the dance floor this early. The party was just getting started! I jumped up and said, "Guuuurrrrl it's muh jam!"

Now, let me remind you we were sitting at the end of the very first table. There were literally seventy-five people sitting in rows behind us, watching our dance skills (we were right next to the dance floor). I'm not the best dancer in the world, but you throw on some good '80s tunes and suddenly I think I'm Carlton from The Fresh Prince with my smooth moves.

As I jumped up and began to shake my booty, doing my best Carlton, a man walked behind me and tugged on the back of my dress. I turned around ready to deck the guy, (ok, not really, but I was truly offended that he yanked on my dress), I mean dude, you saw me sitting with my husband! I whipped around and looked at him, with a look that said, "What are you doing to me?" He looked at me, cracking up laughing, and proceeded to tell me (through his cackling) that the back of my dress had been tucked inside my girdle (aka Spanx) and he was fixing it for me. Almost every person saw my Spanx covered butt hanging out of the dress and showing off my cheeks!

I had to act fast. I knew I had a few choices and needed to make a split second decision. I could either totally freak out and duck under the table and hide there the rest of the night. I could allow my embarrassment to force me to leave and not come back. Ooooooooor I could just keep dancing.

I chose to keep dancing.

So often, life throws some crazy stuff at you. Sometimes it's funny. Often it's humiliating. You want to hide from the world and feel like never showing your face again. And other times, it's so emotionally debilitating that you want to hide under the blankets for days or weeks on end.

No matter what circumstances life throws at you, ultimately it's your choice how you respond. You have been given power and authority over darkness through Jesus Christ. So will you hide and run from the world? Or will you lift your head high and dance anyway?

Honestly, where do you find more joy? Hiding from the world? Or dancing like nobody's watching? There's no joy in hiding. There might be comfort, but that's not joy. Joy is your spirit coming alive when your flesh says to quit.

That night at the wedding, my flesh wanted to go hide. But my spirit said to dance. And dance I did. All. Night. Long.

For the record, that night ended up being one of the best nights of my life.

I believe it's important to tell you that I continued laughing so hard (all night) that I had pee dripping down my leg on numerous occasions. The spot on the back of my dress went from the size of a medium pizza, to the size of a large watermelon, and you know what? I STILL kept dancing!

My husband and I may have only been the only sober ones at that wedding, but we probably looked the drunkest. He couldn't stop laughing, I couldn't stop peeing, and we both kept dancing.

That night will forever stand out in my mind.

You know why?

Because I decided to throw all the worry from every negative circumstance out the window and chose to be joyful.

It clearly wasn't the perfect night. I mean, who in their right mind, goes to a wedding hoping to urinate all over themselves? No one that I know. And I know some pretty crazy peeps. So, nope, it was definitely not ideal.

And yes, I probably should've worn something more than a pantyliner and Spanx. I probably should've worn a darker color, or pants instead of a dress...or maybe tried out a pair of those new wet-proof undies. But hindsight is always twenty-twenty.

The world of should'ves, if onlys, and what ifs can paralyze us. They can keep us from living in the present moment—even the best moments that don't include wetting yourself. I'm talking about those moments of pure bliss. Those two words "What if" can rob you of a glorious moment that will last a lifetime.

I don't live in the What ifs. I choose to live in the What is. And that night, I had to remind myself of What is.

Truth be told, it could be very likely that people thought I'd spilled water all over myself. Who knows right? I mean, it's possible.

Here's the deal though...people are going to think what they want to think no matter what I say or do. I can't control the lens in which they view me, but I can control what they see. And those people at that wedding reception saw a forty-something woman rocking out in a wet dress having an absolute BLAST!

No matter what happens, people will view life through their own lens. You can't control their perception, you can only control your behavior. Own your glorious, messy, magnificent, human self— the good, bad, ugly, and beautiful and rock on anyway!

Jesus loves this mess of a girl... and if He loves me, you should know that He loves your amazing and messy self too!

Bottom Line—

When the enemy comes in trying to kill the melody of joy in your life, choose to keep dancing. Even if the melody stops, dance anyway. The devil can try to stop the melody but if you keep dancing the song will keep playing in your heart.

When we choose to skip the "What ifs" and live in the "What is" or the "Even if, "we can make the best of the present moment without regret. And when you do so, you can make great memories, which end up being phenomenal stories to share!

I challenge you...rid your vocabulary of words like "What if" "If only" "Should have".

"What if" is a statement of fear.

"What is" is a statement of fact.

"Even if" is a statement of faith.

I prefer fact and faith over fear any and every day!

APPLICATION

When fear grips you, instead of looking at the what if's, look at what really is. Then focus in on God and how good He is. Then you'll be able to see that even if _____ (fill in the blank with your worry), God is still God and will sustain you. Choose a verse that speaks to your spirit about this and every time you think about the what if's, let that scripture rebuke them.

Check out this story from Daniel 3. The king was commanding everyone to bow down to him. There were three dudes who loved God so much they wouldn't worship this king. The what ifs didn't matter. In fact, the punishment for not worshipping the king was, no joke, to be thrown into a burning furnace.

These guys chose to stand strong (they kept dancing, if you will) knowing it could cost them their lives. Still they practically dared the king to throw them in the fire and said this, "If we are thrown into the blazing furnace, the God we serve is able to deliver us from it, and he will deliver us from Your Majesty's hand. *But even if he does not,* we want you to know, Your Majesty, that we will not serve your gods or worship the image of gold you have set up."

No matter the outcome, even in death, they knew God would sustain them. *Spoiler alert* They were thrown into the fire! BUT God showed up in the furnace and they came out alive without a singe! Meanwhile, those that opened the furnace were burned up by the heat. Chew on that a minute!

Let's make it personal...

How often is your head filled with thoughts of "What If"?

Do your "What If's" keep you from living your life to the fullest? Do they keep you from dancing and enjoying life?

I challenge you to begin to change your "What If's" to "What is". How does this change your perspective?

When you're struggling with anxiety, it's very easy to get paralyzed by "What if" and shifting to "What is" may not feel like enough. When that happens, I challenge you to shift your thought process and begin to praise your way through. God "even if" the worst happens, I will still serve you because I know you will carry me through. Instead of feeding your fear, begin to feed your faith. While you can't do it on your own, you CAN do it with the strength of the Holy Spirit in you.

Chapter 20

Anticipation Is Greater Than Realization

It's Not as Bad or as Good as You Think It Will Be

Have you ever had an eye appointment where they test your eye pressure? Basically, they puff a small amount of air into your eye to measure the pressure on your eyeballs. I had it done a few months ago and the sweet girl conducting my exam said, "Hold still for just a moment while I do this, and stare over my left shoulder." As I stared, she lifted this little vertical squirt gun looking thing up to my eye. And you know what I did? I blinked over and over again in anticipation of a small, painless puff of air. The anticipation of the puff was beyond worse than the puff itself.

The other day I had to bake something for school and I was in a hurry (judge me if you must, but my life can be a bit chaotic and I needed a shortcut) so I decided to make cinnamon crescent rolls instead of the homemade cinnamon rolls I had signed up for. I ran up to the store and bought about six tubes of the dough. You know, those tubes of dough wrapped in cardboard with metal on each end? If you've ever opened tubed crescent rolls or biscuits you know that as you unwrap the liner sometimes they pop open. As I was unwrapping the liner, my eyes were blinking really fast. In anticipation of the "pop" I held the tube as far away from my body as I could. And don'tcha know that my blinking was all in vain? Nothing popped. Which was the worst, because I had to force it to pop by hitting it on the counter. So, there I was hitting the middle of the tube over the corner of the countertop, and pulling my head as far away as possible. The pop finally came and then I had to do it five more times. Each time, while I knew I wasn't going to get hurt, I still reluctantly opened the container with the expectancy of the pressure releasing. That anticipation and expectation was way worse than the actual burst itself.

Growing up, my dad always used to slowly say in his deep voice, "You two shut it off," which meant quit fighting. He also used to tell us in that same voice, "Anticipation is greater than realization." He was basically saying that what you're expecting is worse than reality. Little did I know how much I would need those words later in life. However at the time, he was usually talking about something like getting a shot at the doctor's office, getting a splinter out, or getting in trouble.

This idea that anticipation is greater than realization plays out in all aspects of life, and can even cause us to struggle in areas, if we don't recognize what is happening. For example, as an adult I began to struggle with anxiety. Not your, "Oh I'm a little nervous about standing up in front of people," kind of anxiety, but the type of anxiety that landed me in the ER as I was trying to convince doctors that I was indeed having a heart attack, as you probably remember from a previous chapter. My anxiety was crippling. I struggled with it for a good ten months before I finally agreed to go get help.

I had given anxiety so much power over my life. I was keeping myself in my house, avoiding social gatherings, family events, and even church. I needed to get help to learn to overcome this thing that was torturing me.

If you've never struggled with anxiety, there's no real way to explain it except for the fact that it feels like you're being suffocated. The more you fight to free yourself, the more power you give the beast. Yet you feel like you can't succumb to it, because then you'd feel like you were just giving up. Anxiety is a tricky little liar.

After meds and therapy I learned that my dad was right-- anticipation usually is greater than realization. This truth stands, no matter what the circumstances are.

How many Christmases have I anticipated the picture perfect holiday? Expecting the kids to love every gift? Expecting everyone to get along all day and for nothing to go wrong? Expecting everyone to help out and every detail to go just as planned?

Anticipation is greater than realization.

How many times have I anticipated a conversation to go one way, only to walk away from it frustrated and let down?

Anticipation is greater than realization

When have I anticipated my spouse would meet a need and I felt disappointed because they couldn't?

Anticipation is greater than realization.

Have you ever worked really hard and saved your money for something, and when you bought it, at first it was great, but you thought it would feel even better? This is yet another example of anticipation being greater than realization.

In our earthly life, the journey is far greater than the destination. When we appreciate the view along the way, we get to see all sorts of sights. Unfortunately, our society is teaching us to hurry and get there yesterday. Everything and everyone is always rushed to make things happen.

Have you ever microwaved a piece of roast beef? I'm not talking about reheating leftovers, I'm talking about taking a whole piece of raw meat and throwing it in the microwave to cook. Chances are, if you know anything about fixing the perfect roast, you know not to do this.

You see, in order to get the perfectly tender, fall-off-the-fork roast, the key is cooking it at a low temperature for a longer amount of time. I typically will put mine in the slow cooker on low before I go to bed, and wake up the next morning to a house that smells of pure roast goodness.

Should I expect to achieve a perfect fall-off-the-fork roast if I'm cooking it in a microwave? HECK NO! While the microwave might get the roast to the right temperature really quickly, it's going to be tough, chewy, and will likely be similar to gnawing on a piece of rubber tire.

When you are expecting slow cooker results from a minute in the microwave, you will be let down. Every. Single. Time.

A microwave is great for reheating a quick snack or for grab and go. But a home cooked meal in the slow cooker will fill you up. It takes time, instructions, care, and effort.

Expectations will steal your joy!

Expectations tend to be demanding.

Expectations tend to be ungrateful.

Expectations are often unrealistic and not easy to achieve.

Expectations will often leave you feeling disappointed.

The anticipation of the expectation can sneak up on relationships and slowly suffocate the relationship to death, without you even knowing it. It's like carbon monoxide poisoning, there are few symptoms, and unless the problem is identified and treated immediately it can be lethal.

I'm going to give you five ways expectation sets you up for emotional devastation. Any one of these can bring about emotional overwhelm on their own. Combine them and the overwhelm is inevitable.

1. You have this expectation as to how things should go. *You expect a specific result. When that expectation isn't met* and the desired outcome isn't realized, *you become overwhelmed.* You then put MORE pressure on yourself to do *whatever* it takes to bring about your original desired outcome and in turn, bring about more overwhelm. (There's a cycle there, do you see it?) You expect to have control over everything in your life. Here's the reality. *No one has any control over anything but themselves.* The irony here is that many people have lost emotional control of themselves because they're spending so much energy trying to control everything/one around them.

2. *The expectations others have put on you.* There are expectations put on you from your co-workers,

your boss, your spouse, your parents, your children, and pretty much any person you have a close relationship with. *Overwhelm occurs when you submit yourself to everyone else's demands while neglecting your needs.*

3. *Expecting someone else to fix a situation for which you feel they are responsible.* When they don't, you feel overwhelmed, frustrated and let down.

4. *You expect to fail.* Your anticipation of a negative outcome puts you in the mindset to receive a negative outcome. This can make you feel miserable and stuck. You've lost hope and that leads to overwhelm.

5. *You expect yourself to be perfect. You are putting unrealistic expectations on yourself (goes along with fixing everything in #1)* And when you turn out to be human, your shortcomings leave you feeling like you're not good enough and you feed your fear rejection. Another recipe for overwhelm.

APPLICATION

Here are three tips to prevent emotional overwhelm.

1. *Get rid of expectations!* Yes, you heard me right. You just read about how expectations can jack you up. Everything you've ever thought you knew about expectations, throw it all out the window! Expectations = Pressure. Let. It. Go. Re-evaluate what is important. Instead of expectations, practice setting standards. When you have a standard of excellence (not to be mistaken for perfection), you aim for a higher level of performance, yet without so much pressure.

2. *Let go of perfection.* If you are seeking perfection in everything you do, you will constantly have a feeling of frustration and you'll never be able to celebrate the beauty of what is going well... because perfection isn't realistic. The expectation of perfection is the greatest thief of any sense of achievement or growth. I encourage you to aim for a level of excellence— which means doing things with a high standard but without expecting perfection!

3. *Realize you have very little to no control over life.* It's said that 10% of life is what happens and 90% is your response to it. So while you can't control what's going on around you, **you can control your response to it.** How do you implement a positive response? The moment you begin to feel tension from a situation, I want you to take a deep breath and take a moment to begin to process whether you want to make this situation work for you, or against you. It's all in your response. If you want to control your emotional overwhelm, you RESPOND to life's situation after thinking through the situation and instead of REACTing in emotion.

Now let's make it personal…

Where in your life has the anticipation been greater than the realization? Give some examples and how that changed your way of thinking (good or bad).

When you read the list of 5 ways expectations set you up for emotional overwhelm, what stood out in your mind?

Where in your life, then, do you need to get rid of expectations and replace them with standards of excellence?

What is the consequence if the standards are not met?

Are you able to offer yourself, as well as those close to you, grace to relieve the emotional toll that expectations are having on you?

How can you offer grace to those in need of it (girl, maybe the one you need to show grace to is that one you see in the mirror!)? What does that look like?

Here are two sweet, yet powerful, little verses I pray over you, dear sister, as you begin to release all of that unwanted pressure and expectation that has had it's grasp on you:

"Therefore I...beg you to lead a life worthy of your calling, for you have been called by God. Always be humble and gentle. Be patient with each other, making allowance for each other's faults because of your love."

Ephesians 4:1-2

Chapter 21

Joy Can Be Bought

Superficial Joy vs. Authentic Joy

{I stand up, move my feet forward to step up on my soapbox and start my Billy Graham style street corner preaching. Please don't hesitate to give me some "Amens", "Preach it girl", and "Come on now." Imma need my amen corner from the church for this chapter.}

I'm going to introduce you to the two types of good feels. The first is what I'm going to refer to as superficial joy. It's that feeling of pleasure when you get a great bargain on that expensive pair of shoes you have been dying to get. It's like a moment of utter bliss! That's superficial joy, muh ladies. It can totally be bought because, well, SHOES! Authentic joy, though, is completely different. It can't be bought because it's so much deeper. It comes from being in a right relationship with God. It's knowing that the creator of the universe loves you so much, he saw fit to send his only son to save YOU! And it's knowing that no matter how bad a situation looks or feels, the same God that created the heavens, the earth and you, is moving at the core of it all.

Superficial joy is your flesh.

Authentic joy is your spirit.

So if you want instant gratification, then go feed your flesh and you will have superficial joy. I remember a famous athletic brand had an advertising campaign that said "Just Do it!" While the world might think that campaign means they should go find their [superficial] joy, as believers, we don't buy into it. We weren't created to for this type of happiness. Instead we were created to be holy. In other words, we weren't created to feed our flesh, we were created to be more like Christ. And in that holiness, we will find peace and joy, which runs so much deeper than any feeling, from even the best external circumstance.

Let me preach real quick for ya here...

Superficial joy is external.

Authentic joy is internal.

Superficial joy is getting what you want.

Authentic joy is appreciating what you have.

Superficial joy is loving the good stuff in your life.

Authentic joy is embracing the trials knowing they serve a greater purpose.

Superficial joy is serving yourself.

Authentic joy is serving others.

Superficial joy is circumstantial.

Authentic joy is contentment of the heart.

Superficial joy can be created.

Authentic joy is acquired.

Superficial joy is conditional.

Authentic joy is unconditional.

Superficial joy does not live with pain.

Authentic joy thrives regardless of pain.

Superficial joy comes from the heart of man.

Authentic joy comes from love of God.

Superficial joy is a feeling.

Authentic joy is a state of mind.

Superficial joy is temporary.

Authentic joy is lasting.

Superficial joy is your flesh.

Authentic joy is your spirit.

Society says joy is an inside job. Yet, at the same time, they are throwing the most "ideal" outside circumstances and consumerism in our faces telling us that's what is going to make us happy. Because we can buy their version of [superficial] joy. Their version of joy is a temporary feeling that is fleeting. We can't, however, buy authentic joy.

{Jumps up on tippy toes to get higher on the soap box}

I'm so tired of hearing that you're responsible for your happiness. Yes, you are responsible for your attitude, and you're responsible for your response to the crazy things life (and people) throw at you. And yeah, that all affects your mood. But can I break it down for you real quick???

Why should we settle for some watered down, diluted version of true joy? There's so much more to living this life than just feeling good. Do I want you to live a life of joy? HECK yeah! But a life of superficial joy?

Girl, let me clear something up for you right now...

Life isn't about being happy and feeling good. It's about being holy. When we decide we want to pursue instant gratification, we will fall for lies of the flesh, or as one of my sons called it, "The Myth of Happiness".

If I just get this job...

If I could just get financially stable...

If I could just get married...

If I were finally able to have kids...

If I could just lose these last ten pounds...

The list goes on and on.

Chase that goal and once you get it you'll be happy. You chase, you get it, and while it's exciting for a moment, the excitement is fleeting. There's no contentment. I don't need Satan to tempt me with jack crap, my flesh is enough to throw me under.

Can I get a witness?

My role as a believer is not to pursue feeling good or being happy. It's to pursue Christ. And in that pursuit He is going to give me a desire to be more holy. And as I continue to pursue Him and live in His presence I will find joy. Superficial joy is circumstantial, authentic joy is relational. When we're in a right relationship with our Creator, we know authentic joy. When we are living up to His holy standard, there is true joy. When we are aligned in His will, even if we're facing great challenges, there is still a peaceful joy.

As believers and followers of Christ, we must FIRST know and believe that our lives are not our own. So, because of this, happiness is not our goal. Holiness is. And when we're holy, we're whole and we'll have an everlasting joy. Feeling good and being happy all the time is a load of crap that society fed us growing up and the enemy is still trying to that feed that lie to us. Yes, I want to be happy. But honestly, that imitation superficial joy is circumstantial. It can change. Holiness is what we're to aim for. When we shoot for holiness, the result is true joy that comes from God alone.

When we're aiming for holiness we're aiming for His presence and we know that in His presence there is fullness of joy.

How about an amen and a Hallelujah right there???

My big haired high school pic in the yearbook was great. It was 1990 and I was the classic late '80s early '90s girl, with all the right clichés signed in my yearbook.

Reach for the stars and you'll go far.

Aim for the sky and you'll go high.

You can do anything you put your mind to.

Work hard and keep pushing, anything is possible.

While yes, we need to work hard, and we need to believe in what we're doing, it's more than just that. It's knowing who you are in Christ and what He has called you to.

I used to think more about my dreams than my calling. I look back to my junior high and high school days and remember when my dream was to be a singer. I desperately wanted a record deal and I had it in my head that I was going to one day sign with a label, go on tour, and live this fancy life of fame and fortune. That dream lasted until I was about twenty-two. I mean come one, just cause I could sing a little karaoke didn't mean I could fill a stadium! Then, I realized that while it was a cool dream, it wasn't God's plan for my life. I was pursuing things that made an earthly impact, not an eternal impact.

When you're chasing after earthly things, they usually fulfill the lust of the flesh. Meaning, they feel good in the moment. However, that feeling doesn't last, and in fact it leaves you longing for more. There's a void that's empty and that place is only for God. When you're constantly running toward the things that make YOU happy you'll always feel empty afterward, because filling your flesh with natural things will always leave you thirsty for more. God is the only thing that will truly quench that thirst in your soul, and the more you try to quench that thirst with things other than Him, the thirstier you become.

It's like being super dehydrated. You're dying for a drink, and someone offers you an ice cold soda. Sure, it might taste good for a moment, but it doesn't really quench your thirst, instead it actually causes more dehydration and leaves you thirstier than you were before. After chasing my dreams and finding my soul empty and dry, I finally ran to the One whose well never runs dry.

I realized that there was something different in store for me, although I didn't know what it was right away. So I kept singing, except only in church now. God's plan didn't have me singing in bars, on TV shows, or at festivals. I wasn't created to chase fame, money, or man's applause and approval. God created me to pursue Him. And when I did that, things began to shift. God had me dancing and doing choreography for our youth choir at church. This was so small compared to what I thought I wanted, yet it was so much more rewarding. Little did I know, He was just getting started.

I'm not telling you to give up on your dreams. I'm simply urging you to surrender your dreams to Him.

When I surrendered my dreams— I traded my goals and the pursuit of what I thought would bring real joy in exchange for pursuing Him. This meant submitting to His will and plan for my life. While I stopped pursuing the dream of one day getting a record label contract, I never stopped pursuing God. The more I pursued God, the more my heart changed and I began longing after something totally different. It was like a new dream was born. I didn't focus on that dream though, I continued to focus on serving the Lord in my day-to-day life. And as long as I was pursuing God on a daily basis, I knew that I was walking out the steps that would ultimately lead me to His plan and purpose. Can I tell you that where I'm at now is far greater than anything I'd have ever dreamed for myself? I'm not famous (in man's eyes) but I'm known and loved by God. That's what matters to me. There's no amount of man's applause that can compete with God's presence. What I do, I do for Him and Him alone.

By the way, it's not been all daisies and roses. I've gotten quite a few thorns along the way. But they've been worth every ounce of pain. Because all those things, both good and bad, have led me here to you today.

I remember working with a client. She was going through a quarter-life-crisis. If you're not familiar with this term, it's when you're somewhere between twenty-two to twenty-five years old and you feel like you should know what you're going to do with your life. College is completed and you have a job (hopefully in your field of choice) but yet life feels empty.

As I sat across from my young client, who had everything in the world going for her, she cried. She was at a loss because she felt like God had something big for her and she needed to figure it out.

I shared with her what I'd learned from experience.

When you're following God daily, you don't have to worry about tomorrow. You fulfill the call He has on your life today and your future will unfold in front of you. And then one day you will look back to see where He has brought you, how He got you there, and how each obstacle was not a roadblock, but a building block to where you are today.

When we look to scripture and read the story of Joseph in Genesis we know that he had a dream, and it was a huge dream. His own brothers did the unthinkable and went against him, threw him in a pit, and ultimately sold him into slavery. Talk about an unhappy situation! However, from the pit to the palace, Joseph continued to walk in obedience every step of the way. That's what led him to his dream. He submitted to the Lord daily and as he walked in the plan God had for him, each step he took directed him to fulfilling that dream that God had given him. I'm sure Joseph's journey didn't look at all like what he had in mind when he had his original dream. However, God's plan and provision got him to the palace and his dream came true. I would guess that there were days when Joseph felt lost. He likely doubted, wondered, and even felt as if he should give up on his dream. But Joseph surrendered his dream as he continued walking with God and pursuing God daily, not his dream. And low and behold, the daily steps led him to the realization of the dream he had as a child.

My sweet sister. I get it. You feel lost. You don't know His plan for your life, but you feel a divine call and desperately want to know what to do next. I want to encourage you to just live in the moment right now and do what He has called you to do today. Your steps have been ordered by the Lord. Nothing and no one that comes against you will deter you from where He wants to take you. Even if you take a misstep, His GPS will recalculate to get you back on track to your divine destination.

You want success? You want joy? You want to live a life that is full?

Pursue God and God alone. He knows the desires of your heart and will give them to you as He sees fit. When you pursue God and a relationship with Him, it will result in a life of Holiness and contentment. Be grateful for every blessing that sits in front of you today and everything He has given you in the past (including challenges!). When you're content, you don't need to be happy. Contentment is a state of mind; superficial joy is a feeling. And we know that feelings can and will lie to us.

So I urge you today my sweet sister, don't give up on your dream-- surrender it. Allow God to move in a way that you can't! Whether He realigns your dream or gives you a new one, I promise you that the joy it will bring will surpass any earthly accolades, satisfaction, or superficial joy you could've ever imagined! Give your life to Him and trust Him with it, because whatever He does, whatever mountains He moves, every river He carries you across, every pit that He pulls you out of, you'll know beyond a shadow of a doubt that it was all for His purpose. And let me tell ya girlfriend, living out His purpose and plan is greater than ANYTHING we could ever even begin to imagine!

Maybe you thought you'd end up filling a stadium and you find yourself filling a sippy cup instead. Know that what God is seeing isn't your broken dreams, but His calling being fulfilled. So as long as you're living a life for Him, it doesn't matter how small it looks in the eyes of man. When you're being obedient, you're living the largest life there is. When you live a life that humbly seeks and serves the King of Kings and the Lord of Lords, your fame and fortune will not be here on earth. Your fame and fortune is eternal.

APPLICATION

Pursue holiness and your relationship with Christ. Walk in the call that He has given you today and do not worry about tomorrow. As you're obedient He will get you where you need to go. As you submit your life to Him, you'll find joy...even in the midst of the darkest trials. Don't believe me? Look it up! Go to John 15:10-11. Sister, this is from a man who doesn't break His promises!!!

Now let's make it personal…

Do you want instant, superficial joy or do you want authentic, sustained joy?

Look at your life, based upon your day to day decisions, are you in pursuit of happiness or holiness?

What changes do you need to make in order to pursue holiness?

How will living a life of holiness change your life?

What is your dream?

Are you willing to surrender your dream to God in pursuit of Him instead of your dream?

At the end of your life here, you will leave behind a legacy. What do you want that legacy to be?

How can you live a life that will honor that legacy while being true to who God has called you to be?

Epilogue

It's that time. The end of the book. We've laughed, we've cried, and I've rapped a line or two. Thank you for taking this journey with me. I actually had a twenty-second chapter written and ended it with scripture. But to be honest, the words I wrote in the chapter fell short. So I want to close with this, which I believe sums it all up:

We have joy because of our Heavenly Father. He is at the root of it all.

"Though you have not seen him, you love him; and even though you do not see him now, you believe in him and are filled with an inexpressible and glorious JOY." 1 Peter 1:8

May you continue to pursue Him, my friend. He is everything you need and more.

225

Acknowledgements

First let me start with you, the reader. I want to thank you for your support—through buying, reading, and sharing this book...not to mention all the love you've given me on social media. Much like a tree falling in the woods, with no one around, it doesn't matter if it makes noise. Without you, these are merely words on a page but because of your reading, they make "noise." I trust it is helpful noise and that the Lord uses this to speak encouragement and healing to your heart. This book is a dream come true and you helped make it a reality. Thank you!

I am grateful to my teammates who were with me through this process. First, my editor Melissa. You allowed me to keep my voice, and my crazy stories. Your insight to pause and get feedback when things my have been a bit bold was gold. You put my mind at ease and let me know I'm "normal" when second guessing everything. And you put up with all my last minute changes while I was trying to put my perfectionist tendencies to rest. You are a top notch editor. Thank you. Jason Moore. A teammate I didn't know I needed but God did. Dude, you have been a tremendous blessing. You've answered questions, connected me with people who could help guide me through this process, whipped up awesome graphics and have been a phenomenal resource. You're a great guy with a fantastic wife that works behind the scenes as you help people like me, so thanks to Michele as well. You two are a blessing. Thanks for generously sharing your time and your talents.

To my other teammate, my rockstar of a "Social Media Strategist" turned "Assistant" who is so much more than an assistant. There's no label for you, Amy Klassen. All I can say is that you are priceless. Girl, you mentioned something about me writing a book when we first met and I jawed back at you telling *you* to write one. I'm so sorry— I was totally kidding… kinda! Now months (that have felt like years) later, here we are. You've been along my side for the topsy-turvy ride that would make most people so motion sick they'd have jumped. But not you. The shakier things got, the more you stuck by my side, praying for me and being there to fix whatever I couldn't. You helped lighten my load to make things happen. And grateful is beyond an understatement. I just know that God planted you right here, and I'm so glad you bloomed right where he planted you.

When undertaking your first book, especially when it wasn't something you really planned to do, it can really mess with your mind. Does this matter? Do people really care what I have to say? Who really wants to read this anyway? Those of you who asked, to my friends (in person and on social media) and family who checked in or sent messages of encouragement about the book, while you may not have realized it, you kept me writing. You kept this book alive. You were keeping me accountable and made me believe that it was my own personal field of dreams..."If I write it, they will order it." You made me feel like my book mattered and constantly reminded me that I had words someone not only wanted, but needed to hear. You kept me writing on days when I felt like I may not have anything to say. To those who generously shared their time and insight, I'm grateful for you as well. To the ones who took their precious time to proofread, to review, and to share feedback, thank you. It reassured me that this is infact a project that would be worth the blood, sweat, and tears.

To muh girl, my soul sisda Krista Kokot. You have been there for it all the last couple of years. You helped pick me up when I was stuck on my couch in PJs and a cast. You gave me pep talks when I needed them. You reminded me what I had to write mattered and that I needed to get it down on paper. You kept me laughing and in the midst of your busy life, still made time for me.

You are a phenomenal friend and an equally phenomenal coach. I love you my sweet sister. Your words, your support, your sisterhood, and your understanding, are what make you a rare gem to be treasured. I'm forever thankful that the Lord chose you to be my roomie that fateful weekend in NJ.

And then there are my sisters. Heather, Heidi, and Rachel. You girls. You listened to me about this book a million times and never told me to shut up. You read the chapters countless times and always made me feel like I could do this thing. And you did it in the midst of the busyness of your own lives. You've believed in me. Always. Not just in this book venture, but also in everything I've ever done. I really believe that when God gave me you three as my sisters, he handpicked the best ones just for me. Thank you for understanding when I couldn't be somewhere or when I couldn't be "present" at different functions because I was working on this thing. I couldn't have given birth to this book without your support. I'm forever grateful for you crazy girls— who keep me humble and tell me what's up, especially when I need corrected and need to hear the bold truth. I'm honored to be grouped in with you as one of those "Bowman Girls."

To my boys. All four of you were around when joy wasn't so much my jam. Through the years you have brought so much joy to my life and you've reminded me countless times to choose joy in the smallest things. To my younger two still at home, you have been amazing at putting up with me as I've written this thing. You've made meals, gone grocery shopping, done housework, and gotten me out of my office so that I didn't forget to live a life while writing. You've put up with my moments of stress, and you've encouraged me to keep going when I felt like quitting. You constantly speak words of life into every aspect of what I do. And more than anything, you have expressed how proud you are that I'm following the Lord's leading, no matter how crazy it might seem or how embarrassing it might be to you! I hope all you boys know how much I love you and that my continued prayer is that I live out an example of love, grace, and joy, so that you may live that way also. I love each one of you. Thank you all for being you.

To my amazing husband. Steve Semih Mutlu. From the moment we met, you have brought out the best in me and made me feel like I could do absolutely anything. You have always let me shine. You've helped fuel my shine when it began to dim. When I lost my confidence or fight, you've jumped in and fought for me. You put up with me being obnoxious and getting crazy with my sisters. You encourage me to be me 100% me, loving me for it all. Even the ugly stuff nobody else sees. You allowed me to share some deeply personal, and sometimes comical, stories about our lives, not just in the book, but in coaching, in speaking, in preaching or any time someone else could benefit from our crazy stories. You've never once elbowed me under the table for sharing "too much." Thank you for giving me permission to share more than what people should know about our lives. Yet, you do it willingly to help others.

There are many things in my adult life that would not exist if I didn't have you. The kids, the family, the memories, the stories (including the countless funny stories that aren't in the book), my career, and the unending support. Thank you for walking me through every leg of our journey, and carrying me when necessary. Sometimes following the Lord isn't easy, in fact it's been the exact opposite, however, we still follow him together...even when it doesn't make sense to others. Thank you for walking beside me through it all. You exemplify the love of Christ in so many ways. I'm humbled that you choose me daily, that you see the best in me and that you stick by me at my worst. Thank you for believing in me enough to be my business partner, loving me enough to be my life partner, and giggling with me enough to be my giddy partner. The night that we met, you told me that you were one in a million. Over the years, you've proved that wrong—you're not one in a million, you're one in a lifetime. Thank you for being unapologetically you. I love you more today than yesterday, but not as much as tomorrow.

To my parents— all of you. We epitomize the modern day blended family. It really does take a village and not when your kids are just kids, but when they're adults too. You have impacted me in ways that have shaped and molded me into who I am today. I'm appreciative of all the obstacles that were thrown in our way, they helped teach me how to trust the Lord and choose joy...And know that every pain, every mistake, every glorious victory, was all used for the building of the kingdom of God. While table manners and being ladylike (all the time) may not be my strong points, making people laugh and helping women overcome adversity are, and I have you to thank for that. I love you Dad. Thank you for my smile and my warped humor, both are a great weapon in life. Mom, I love you, thank you for showing me the generous heart of Christ, and that I don't need any credit, it all belongs to Jesus. Robyn, thank you for constantly serving and doing and then serving more, even when it hurts. I love you. Dave, thank you for being constant. You're proof that God shows up when we may have given up—and you remind us to laugh through it all. I love you. Baba, I pray that you know the difference you've made in my life, not only while you were here on earth, but also when you went home. Anne, thank you for taking me in as your own. You continue to inspire me, make me laugh (yep, so hard that I wet my pants) and you teach me so much. I do believe that God uniquely created you and Baba to be my extended parents. Each one of you have played and continue to play a unique role in my life. Words can't express how grateful I am that God chose each one of you to love on me and pour into me. I love you all more than you'll ever know.

ABOUT THE AUTHOR

Christian Counselor, Speaker, & Author, Holly Mutlu has served in almost every aspect of ministry over the last 25 years. From Sunday School, to women's ministry director, to associate Pastor. In 2009, her desire to help heal the hurting and pour joy into those around her led her to obtain her Bachelor's of Christian Counseling. As a Clinical Member of the NCCA, she has devoted her life to helping women and families overcome the obstacles of circumstance and embrace joy to its fullest.

Holly loves Jesus, watermelon, and anything that sparkles. She never backs down from a chance to shake what her mama gave her or to share the gifts her Heavenly Father gave her. Powered by faith, family, and tacos, she keeps her husband of 20 years on his toes, as they tackle the adventures of parenting 4 young men, creating impromptu music videos, and going from a blog about watermelons to dreams of a best sellers list.

Tap into the infectious joy, and genuine love that is Holly Mutlu on instagram @hollymutlu.